What People Are Saying about Jim Maxim and *Face-to-Face with God*

Jim Maxim is a living testimony of God's power to redeem. His journey will inspire you to trust the Master for release from your captivity.

—Dr. Jack Hayford
Jack Hayford Ministries
Founding pastor, The Church On The Way
Van Nuys, CA

This book is a must-read. Jim's life is a vindication of hope and faith in the relentless love of God. The book contains a treasure chest of theological and biblical truths that do not require a professor of theology to unlock.

—Dr. Herbert H. Lusk II
Pastor, Greater Exodus Baptist Church
Philadelphia, PA
Former running back, Philadelphia Eagles

Do you believe in miracles and the power of prayer? You will after reading the story of Jim Maxim's encounter with God.

—Rev. Randy Carroll
Former pastor of fifty years
Findlay, OH

The story of God's amazing grace in the life of Jim Maxim is a testimony to God's sovereign, miraculous, and saving love. Read this book and be blessed. Share his message of hope with others who've lost their way. See again how the gospel of Jesus Christ makes broken lives overflow with strength and joy.

—Dr. Peter A. Lillback
President, Westminster Theological Seminary
Philadelphia, PA

It is one thing to read about God's work in a man's life; it is another to see it lived out. For ten years, I have had that privilege. Jim Maxim's story of a life transformed is one of the great apologetics for belief in the Christian God. Read it and rediscover what grace means.

—Pastor Bob Guaglione
Calvary Chapel of Delaware County
Chadds Ford, PA

Since Jim's first encounter with Christ, he has been faithful to the sacred trust of remaining "face-to-face" with God in the secret place of prayer. He and his wife, Cathy, have provided an oasis for the brokenhearted, from the inner-city of Philadelphia to those in poverty in Nepal.

Jim's amazing personal story of grace brings hope to the hopeless by bringing them "face-to-face" with the One who loves them most.

—Tom Lofton
Founder, 12.12, The Annual Global Day of Prayer
for the Poor and Suffering
Springfield, MO

Life is full of difficulties and trials, but Jim Maxim has learned to live triumphantly because of his walk with God. I have known Jim for more than thirty years and have found him to be a *genuine friend*, a man of integrity who makes an impact for God in the business world, in his family life, and around the world with his passion for souls. I admire him for his boldness and consistency in his witness for Christ.

—Pastor James Leake
Acts 20:24 Ministry
Pastor Emeritus, Monroeville Assembly of God
Monroeville, PA

Jim Maxim is a pillar of strength for God's kingdom, living his faith practically. I commend his powerful story of desperation transformed into redemption.

—Dr. Keith Phillips
President, World Impact, Inc.
Los Angeles, CA

Jesus showed His passion, compassion, and resolve time and again during His earthly journey. Jim Maxim, with an inspiring and prayer-filled awe for the Lord, has discovered the power of those same emotions in following the Spirit's leading as a Christian witness in his own journey. Readers of this book will be inspired to follow similarly.

—David R. Black, Ph.D.
President, Eastern University
St. Davids, PA

To Mom

FACE TO FACE WITH GOD

JIM MAXIM

WHITAKER
HOUSE

FACE-TO-FACE WITH GOD
A True Story of Rebellion and Restoration

Jim Maxim
Acts413
P.O. Box 628
Southeastern, PA 19399
www.acts413.net
610-721-1010

ISBN: 978-1-60374-286-3
Printed in the United States of America
© 2011 by Jim Maxim

Whitaker House
1030 Hunt Valley Circle
New Kensington, PA 15068
www.whitakerhouse.com

Library of Congress Cataloging-in-Publication Data
Maxim, Jim, 1953–
  Face-to-face with God / Jim Maxim.
    p. cm.
  Summary: "This personal account of Jim Maxim's deliverance from alcoholism and a destructive lifestyle after a near-fatal car accident, when Jesus appeared to him and gave him a second chance at life, shows how readers can receive God's love and purpose for living"—Provided by publisher.
  ISBN 978-1-60374-286-3 (trade pbk. : alk. paper) 1. Conversion—Christianity. 2. Maxim, Jim, 1953—Childhood and youth. I. Title.
  BV4921.3.M29 2011
  243—dc22
                                        2011011231

1 2 3 4 5 6 7 8 9 10 11 **W** 18 17 16 15 14 13 12 11

Contents

ACKNOWLEDGMENTS

To Cathy, my wife of thirty-five years: I would like to thank you for all the years of being my number one fan. Only you know the song of my heart, and, many times, you sang it back to me when I forgot the words. I would not be the man I am without you. You have a personal walk with God that I have seen up close, and it has inspired me deeply. I love you with all my heart.

To my sons, Jim, John, and Jordan; my daughters-in-law, Alison, Lauri, and Jesica; and my grandchildren, Lucy, James, and Dylan. My deepest desire for you is that you walk humbly with God and place Him first in your lives, always. I love you.

To Vicki Mlinar, my friend, my sister-in-law, and my sister in Christ, as well as my editor: Thank you for keeping me on track with this story and making sure we kept Jesus and His love for the lost its main focus. Vicki, you are truly a woman of God, and watching you trust God and walk with Him in the way you do is awesome. You have always sought to honor God, and I know you make Him proud of you.

To Bob Whitaker Jr., of Whitaker House: Your desire to reach the lost and keep the tip of your compass pointed to Christ will continue to further the kingdom of God. I know it will be said of you, "Well done, good and faithful servant. Enter into the joy of your Lord." Bob, you always were a class act. Thanks.

To Lois Puglisi, my sister in Christ and final editor: Without your patience and gentle prodding for me to think everything through thoroughly, this story would not have been complete. Your desire for excellence to give God your very best has inspired me deeply and made this story of redemption more effective for God to use to reach the lost and encourage His people. Lois, you have always given God your best, and it shows in all you do. Thank you.

FOREWORD

The first time I met Jim Maxim, I felt a kindred spirit with him! However, I felt like I'd already met him from reviewing his manuscript. It is a powerful and compelling story. I highly recommend it.

In some ways, Jim's testimony is like those I have witnessed in over fifty years of ministry to the addicted population through Teen Challenge, founded by my brother David Wilkerson, where I have ministered all my adult life. Beginning with Nicky Cruz's conversion, I have seen literally thousands of miracles of dramatically changed lives.

Jim had a similar encounter with God. Alcohol almost destroyed him. Yet, by the sovereign grace of God, Jesus revealed Himself to him as a youth. Jim was raised up from a hospital bed with stitches covering his face after he had been thrown into a windshield during a car accident, and a physical, emotional, and spiritual healing took place in him. Today, he is a successful businessman who tells his redemptive story in the United States and overseas.

I am thankful that Jim has now told his story in the pages that follow. I recommend giving this book to those whom I call the "up-and-outers," as well as to the "down-and-outers" who are touched by some serious life-controlling problem. And, if you are a parent or spouse of someone who is living a destructive lifestyle, read Jim's account of going from within a yard of hell to an incredible new life—it will give you hope.

—Don Wilkerson
President, Teen Challenge, Inc.

PREFACE

Although my mom, Isobel Maxim, stood only five feet two inches, she was definitely one of God's giants in the spiritual realm. She knew God intimately, and, because of that, she wrestled down through prayer the "wicked spirits in high places" for her eight children. She knew what it was to fight for the lives of her children in the spiritual realm because her Lord had taught her that all things are possible through the power of almighty God. Friends of mine who had heard of her prayer ministry and visited her would often say, "From the moment we walked in, the presence of God was so powerful, it was like we were in a holy place."

There is a scene in the book of Revelation, chapter 5, that describes her heart attitude, which is what caused the powers of darkness to release the stronghold they had on me. It reads like this:

Then I looked, and I heard the voice of many angels around the throne, the living creatures, and the elders; and the number of them was ten thousand times ten thousand, and thousands of thousands, saying with a loud voice: "Worthy is the Lamb who was slain to receive power and riches and wisdom, and strength and honor and glory and blessing!" And every creature which is in heaven and on the earth and under the earth and such as are in the sea,

> *and all that are in them, I heard saying: "Bless-*
> *ing and honor and glory and power be to Him*
> *who sits on the throne, and to the Lamb, forever*
> *and ever!" Then the four living creatures said,*
> *"Amen!" And the twenty-four elders fell down*
> *and worshiped Him who lives forever and ever.*
> (Revelation 5:11–14)

If you or a loved one is in a tough situation, and, in the natural, it seems almost impossible that any good can come out of it, my mom would say to you, "This book is for you." It is my prayer that you will enter into the secret place of prayer and into the very presence of God. For it is there that all the victories are won, no matter what odds are against you. I am living proof of this reality.

PART ONE

ONE YARD FROM HELL

1

Into the Darkness

I was seated behind the wheel of my 1962 Oldsmobile Dynamic 88. It was December 27, 1971, so the car had seen a few years of scrapes and gashes. And so had I. At eighteen years of age, with high school just six months behind me, I was a well-known brawler, always ready for a party or a fight. That night, I'd had more than a few drinks with my buddies at a party, and I thought I was feeling just perfect.

Stopped at a red light, I popped the tape out of my eight-track player. I was ready for a new song. I reached across to my glove box to get a different tape. *The Chicago Transit Authority* would be perfect for the buzz I was feeling. The tape slipped from my fingers and fell to the car floor. I was so drunk that when I bent over to pick it up, I passed out, and my head started dropping to the car seat. Coming to for a brief second, I looked up and saw a car headed in my direction.

He's going to hit me! I screamed silently, then passed out again.

The oncoming car missed me; somehow, I had swung the steering wheel to the left and veered out of its way. Out of control, my Olds flew up an embankment and careened back down again. The front of my car smashed with a sickening *crunch* into a dark, looming telephone pole.

CRASHING THROUGH THE WINDSHIELD

My face struck the dashboard and my jaw cracked. I hit the windshield like a bullet and crashed through the glass. I was a pretty big guy, even at that age, six feet three inches, so when my shoulders hit the windshield, they were too broad to get through the crack, and they stopped my body from being thrown from the car. But what happened next was the worst part of the nightmare.

The car came to a sudden stop, and the weight of my body pulled me back inside the vehicle with a vengeance. As my head slid back through the windshield, the razor-sharp edges of the broken glass sliced my face wide open. I was thrown down onto the floor on the passenger side, with blood flowing freely from dozens of gashes in my head.

The first policeman on the scene wrenched open the passenger door to reach me. The blood from my face began flowing over the top of his shoe. "I think this is a dead one," the cop shouted to his partner.

"IT'S TOO LATE. HE'S DEAD!"

One of the last things I remember that night was blood and glass flying all around me. I looked up and across the street and saw the local funeral home.

Is that my next stop? I wondered... then remembered nothing more.

> **I saw the funeral home and wondered,** *Is that my next stop?*

It took combined accounts from the police, doctors, nurses, and my mother and sisters to put all the puzzle pieces together for me regarding what happened over the next hours and days.

The ambulance pulled into the emergency room driveway at Columbia Hospital late that night. A policeman opened the back door of the ambulance, took one look at me, and exclaimed to his partner, "Forget it; it's too late. He's dead!"

"I'M STILL WITH YOU"

"No, I'm still with you," I muttered thickly as I looked up from my cot. They were astonished to hear me speak!

I was rushed into the emergency room. It was the Christmas season, and there were no surgeons on duty. The young intern who ran into my hospital room stopped short in horror. As he looked at the bloody mess that was my head and face, he hardly knew where to begin. Feverishly, he tried to stop the bleeding while assessing the damage to my skull.

The cut on the top of my head was deep, so his first concern was the extent of the brain damage. Then, he looked at my eyes and realized that the jagged edges of the glass had cut across both eyes when my body was thrown back into the car. As the blood flow slowed down, the shaken intern began the process of removing bits of glass from my eyes as quickly as possible, while waiting anxiously for the surgeon's arrival. When it became obvious that no one with more experience would be coming to help anytime soon, the intern began to sew the worst cuts on my face closed. Not being a plastic surgeon, he just sewed me shut, doing his best to save my ebbing life.

I struggled in and out of consciousness. When I had first arrived at the hospital, I had kept gasping to the police, "Is everyone else okay?" That had sent them into a momentary panic. Had they missed someone else who had been thrown from the car? I heard them talking as they kept asking me if anyone else had been with me. And then I slipped away...into the darkness.

2

LOST WITHOUT HOPE

The December night of the accident was a cold, snowy one in Pittsburgh, Pennsylvania. I was at the country club's employee Christmas party. I had caddied at that club since the fifth grade, and now I had the "prestigious" job of shining shoes in the men's locker room. The party was great because I could drink all their high-end booze for free, and I was feeling good. I loved Gilbey's and Beefeater gin. It went down so smoothly, and you couldn't smell it very easily, which made it okay to drink just about anytime.

The Christmas party was wonderful, but by the time it ended, I was too drunk to drive home. My buddy Barry drove me in my car, and his girlfriend followed us in his car. I was foolish enough to think that I hadn't had enough fun. As long as I could still walk, I could still party. They made the big mistake of handing me my car keys when they dropped me off. Instead of walking in the front door, I hid on the side of my parents' home until Barry and his girlfriend drove away. Then, I quickly jumped into my car and drove in the opposite direction. I wanted to spend a few more minutes with Mr. Gilbey. *What could it hurt?* I thought.

TRAPPED BY ADDICTION

I was very young when I started to drink. It began one day after school in the eighth grade when I was at my friend's house. Both his parents worked, so we had the place all to ourselves for a few hours. They had bottles of booze in their house, so, we figured, why not have a few drinks? They would never miss it. And, after all, we weren't hurting anyone else; what could be wrong with a few drinks?

Well, after having a taste of feeling that good, I wondered what else was out there. As long as no one was getting hurt, it seemed okay to keep trying new stuff.

For the next five years, I explored as many ways as I could to get high. My caddying friends and some other buddies introduced me to some new "friends"— marijuana, hash, methamphetamines, and the really "cool" one, mescaline. Between the pills and booze, I had started a journey that I would come to regret. But, as a teenager, I thought I was just "having fun" getting high. It also made any problems I had disappear, at least for a little while.

BIG JACK'S IMPACT ON ME

My dad, Jack Maxim, owned a bar called Big Jack's Bar...Famous for Nothing! He was quite the personality—six feet four inches, two hundred eighty-five pounds of muscle, with hands as big as a giant's. Nobody wanted to mess with him! His bar was right next to the corner where I hung out with my drinking buddies.

One night, one of Big Jack's friends walked by our corner. I remember clearly that we all said hi to the guy; he was so drunk that we didn't bother him. But that's not what he told my dad. About fifteen minutes later, we heard some commotion coming from Big Jack's Bar. The streetlight was a little dim, but I knew right away who was thundering our way. It was the drunken guy, with Big Jack looming beside him. We honestly hadn't said anything but hi to him, but he told Big Jack that some punks at the corner had roughed him up a little.

There were about ten of us, and it was pretty dark in the back parking lot where we were standing. Anyone else might have been intimidated, but Big Jack stomped right into the middle of the gang and barked at his friend, "Put your back up against mine!" He looked around intently and then yelled, "All right, you punks. You thought you were tough with one guy; now is your chance to see how tough you really are!"

I had my head down, hoping my dad would not recognize me in the darkness. But when I realized what was about to happen, and that one of my buddies could get hurt, I had to speak out. I got just a few words out—"Dad, we didn't do anything to this guy"—and, before I knew it, that giant right hand slammed across my face and knocked me backward. It wasn't the time to have a father-son talk, so he just told me to get myself home, and he would deal with me later. Right now, he wanted to prove something else to the guys on the corner. Slowly, I walked home, and cooler heads prevailed, but that gives you a glimpse of Big Jack. Life was rough at times, and drinking was a way to make its roughness fade away.

FORGETTING THE PAIN

At first, I got high just to have some fun, but it wasn't long before getting high became the main focus of my life. It never dawned on me that the drugs and alcohol were fast becoming a lifestyle for me. When you're a kid, you never consider that you can become totally dependent on alcohol. The idea of being an alcoholic was ridiculous. Little did I know that five out of the eight kids in my family would suffer from alcoholism, have to go to rehab, and experience continual life failures, or that dysfunction would rule our lives for a very long time.

> Alcohol is very cunning. The thought that you are slowly destroying yourself, not to mention continually causing pain for the people around you, doesn't occur to you.

Alcohol is so very cunning. It tells you that you have no problem, that you're just having a little fun. The thought that you are slowly destroying yourself, not to mention continually causing pain for the people around you, doesn't occur to you.

The idea of my having a "problem" with alcohol just couldn't be real. I knew I loved to drink, and why not? Again, I wasn't hurting anyone, right? Well, that started to change the longer I kept drinking. By this time, many of my friends had begun to stick needles into their arms, and I figured that alcohol was different. I thought, *I'm no junkie. I'm not going to be like that.* I may not have been sticking my veins with needles, but I sure was filling them up—it was just a different drug. It was my drug of choice. I didn't know that I was already addicted. Most alcoholics don't know it until a day arrives for all of them: the day they hit bottom. It's just a matter of time because it's definitely going to happen. The only question is, how much damage is it going to inflict, and will you still be alive the day it happens?

One night, I was driving on the parkway toward downtown Pittsburgh with my friend Dave. We were just out having our usual time. We had a cooler in the backseat filled with beer and wine, we had just finished a few joints, and we were cruising along.

I started to pull out to pass the person in front of me, and I hit the side of his car. The worst part about it was that I didn't even know it. Dave looked over at me and said, "Hey, man, you just hit that guy's car." My response at the time shows you the state of mind I had when I was either drunk or stoned. I looked back at him and said, "So what? He'll never catch me," and I took off down the parkway. I had no regard for the people in the car I had just hit, and I certainly didn't even think about how drunk I was and how what was about to happen could kill a few people, not to mention Dave or myself.

After I took off, I thought that was going to be the end of it. Little did I know that the guy I had hit was an off-duty Pittsburgh police officer. Not only that, but he had his wife in the car, and she was seven months pregnant. As I floored the gas pedal, I just assumed that in a few minutes, it would all be over, and we could just pick up where we had left off and keep on with our party. But the cop had different ideas.

I looked in the rearview mirror and couldn't believe what I saw. This guy really had the nerve to chase me, so I thought I would give him the ride of his life, and that it would be only a few minutes before he was history. Again, the one thing I didn't know was that he was a cop, a *very angry* cop, a *motivated* cop who had his pregnant wife in the car with him.

> Dave started yelling at me to get over to the right because I was driving in the lane for oncoming traffic.

At the end of the parkway, you had to choose either to go straight downtown or to go across one of the many bridges in Pittsburgh. We were headed to the other side of town, so we had to cross a particular bridge. There is a stream of traffic lights right before this bridge, but I just ran all the lights and figured, once more, that this had to be the last of him. As I got closer to the bridge, Dave started yelling at me to get over to the right because I was driving in the lane for oncoming traffic and was headed for the wrong side of the tunnel at the end of the bridge.

I moved to the correct lane, but as we got inside the tunnel, traffic backed up, and Dave said, "He's right there." The cop had pulled to within two car lengths of us and had his badge in his hand, holding it outside his window, screaming, "Stop! Police!" I looked over at him and saw the angry look on his face. Then, the traffic started moving, and I decided to just take off again. I lost him after a few minutes—so I thought. As I would later learn, he was much smarter than I. He had taken down my license plate number while we were in the traffic backup in the tunnel, so this was not the last time I would see that angry face.

A SHORT REPRIEVE

The car I had been driving that night was registered in my dad's name. I can't remember why, but I wasn't living at home for a few days after that incident, and when I returned and walked into my house, my mom said to me, "Jim, your dad's been arrested!" I looked at her and asked, "Well, what did he do now?" She was wearing that look on her face that said, *Are you ever going to be all right?*

Then, she said, "Jim, I don't think he did anything, because the Pittsburgh police came here and took him downtown under arrest for a hit-and-run on a Pittsburgh police officer's vehicle, and his pregnant wife was in the car!" I knew I was busted and could only imagine how it was going to be when I saw Big Jack face-to-face. My mind started going in a million directions, trying to figure out how I could con my way out of this one, but I couldn't come up with any way out.

Big Jack and I had it out, and he wasn't quite sure what to do with me because, after all, he loved to drink, and he sure had his challenges with alcohol, too. With five or six other kids still living at home and the cops coming to arrest him, the situation was a mess, but somehow we got through it, just like all the other times. He went to court with me and met with the judge and police officers privately, and he somehow got them to let me off. He went in there and pleaded my case for me and fought for his kid, in spite of how screwed up I was. When we got back in the car to go home, we had one of those father-son moments. He loved his family and wanted only the best for us, but when alcohol dominates your very existence, it's impossible to be the person you truly want to be. Alcohol takes no prisoners. It will destroy everything in its path. It is relentless.

I'm sure we both felt bad about what had happened, and we knew something had to change, but what? The obvious answer was to "wise up, stop drinking, and change your lifestyle," right? I'm sure I said all the things every alcoholic says: "That's it; I am not going to do that again. I'm really going to watch my drinking. I'm only going to have one or two and leave it at that. Maybe I'll smoke a joint or two, but no more crazy stuff," and on and on and on. I made all the promises to myself, but, the fact is, as long as I was willing to have just one drink, I could never be free from this taskmaster, old man alcohol. Unless I took the right steps to end my relationship with alcohol, it was just a matter of time before someone else—or I—was going to get hurt again.

OUT OF CONTROL

I wanted to share the above incident with you to give you a glimpse into the state of mind I had developed. When I would drink, it wasn't just a social thing for me, even at eighteen. Alcohol certainly controlled me whenever I gave myself to it. I remember times when I would just drive around by myself and get wasted. I never felt alone because, after all, I was talking to the bottle.

There is a poem about alcohol by an anonymous author that really sums up how crafty it is as it plays on people's minds:

> I am more powerful than all the combined armies of the world.
> I have destroyed more men than all the wars of all the nations.
> I have caused millions of accidents and wrecked more homes than all the floods, tornadoes, and hurricanes put together.
> I am the world's slickest thief; I steal billions of dollars each year.
> I find my victims among the rich and the poor alike.
> I am relentless, insidious, unpredictable.
> I bring sickness, poverty, and death.
> I give nothing and take all.
> I am your worst enemy.
> I am alcohol.

Looking back now, I cannot remember a time when I went anywhere with my friends that we didn't get high or drunk. You see, when you're an alcoholic, you don't drink just to drink. You drink to the point where you can't recognize yourself anymore. Deep in your heart, you know that is the reason why you're drinking in the first place. To forget about who you are and the failure of what you've become. Before you know it, there are demons of alcoholism and addiction that are controlling your very soul.

You're trapped—you can't make it in life sober or being the real you. Getting high might not be great, but it's better than facing the reality of life. The drugs, the alcohol—it's your way of dealing with it all. You can bury the pain of the person who looks back at you in the mirror.

Yet, in the back of my mind, there was always an uneasy feeling that my life was out of control. Sometimes, I felt like I was on a train track being pushed down the line, and I couldn't stop or escape. I just hoped that a train wasn't coming from the opposite direction.

That December night—in the anguish of the accident—I met my train head-on, just like I'd feared.

3

THOSE DREADED WORDS

It was two o'clock in the morning, and the quietness of the house was broken by the piercing ring of the telephone. My sister Jane answered the phone cautiously, already thinking, *Oh, no, what is this going to be about? Which one of my brothers is in trouble now?* The voice on the other end of the line said, "This is Columbia Hospital calling. Is this Mrs. Maxim?" As her heart began to sink, Jane said, "No, this is her daughter." Then, the woman, who was a nurse, asked, "How old are you?" Jane told her that she was twenty-one and asked what this was about. The nurse said it was about her brother Jim, who had been in an accident. I can only imagine the thoughts that were running through Jane's mind. She knew my lifestyle.

The nurse then inquired if her mother was home, and Jane asked her to wait a minute because her mother was sleeping, but she would wake her up. Fear clung to her as she hurried into Mom's room to tell her of the phone call and the hospital waiting to speak to her about her son.

My mother answered the phone with fear gripping her heart. "Don't let it be too bad, Lord!" she whispered into the night. "Let them be all right."

"Is this Mrs. Maxim?" a woman's quiet voice was questioning on the other end of the line.

Instantly, Mom's heart sank, too. She had heard similar tones in people's voices before. You know, when a stranger's voice is kind and polite, comforting. Immediately, you are alert. The news you are about to hear is not what you want to hear at all. The tone of voice sets your nerves on edge, and your stomach gets a familiar sick feeling. Like a thick blanket, a fear of the unknown muffles everything around you. Mom braced herself for the worst, silently praying that she would hear the best. *Please, Lord, don't let me hear the word "dead"!*

"Mrs. Maxim, your son Jim has been in a car accident. We need you to come to the hospital right away." For my mother, it was a nightmare that was suddenly real. She desperately wanted to believe she would wake up, that she wasn't really hearing those dreaded words.

Mom knew she would have to go immediately, but her mind was overwhelmed with fear-laden thoughts and frantic emotions. She didn't want to know how bad it was yet. As she battled the fear, she could only shake her head in disbelief. *Not again,* she thought. Phone calls in the night had happened too many times before.

Not again, my mother thought. Phone calls in the night had happened too many times before.

How bad was it this time? Is he alive? Will he be crippled, or worse? Did he hurt or kill someone else in the crash? The fears tore through her consciousness.

What was she going to do now? "Can I wait to come in the morning?" she asked the nurse hopefully. "I'm afraid it would be better if you came right away," was the woman's only response.

Mom's world was crashing in. She knew it had been a serious accident, but she also knew the nurse was purposely withholding some details. She wanted to ask more questions, and yet she didn't. Somehow, it wasn't the time for words. It was time to leave, to see her son, to see if he was still alive. Time to face her greatest fear. She woke Big Jack and told him the news.

My parents arrived at the hospital as the intern was sewing up my face. Gently, the nurses took them aside and explained that they had no idea if I would lose my left eye or not. It had the most damage from glass shards that still remained in it. They explained that my head was injured and there was the possibility of brain damage. It would be some time before they knew anything for certain. All they could do now was wait for the surgeon to come and take me into the operating room to search for answers.

FACING THE FEAR

Why did Mom especially fear receiving nighttime calls? Because she had eight children to care for, and her oldest sons seemed to be bent on just one thing—getting into trouble. My dad wasn't there much to help her with raising us, so my mother did her best to guide us in the right direction. My oldest brother was about twenty-four years old at the time of my accident, and the youngest was just eight. I was the fourth in line, following my two older sisters.

Each day, my mom spent hours in the kitchen preparing meals and cleaning up after us. Faithfully, she would stand at the kitchen sink and pray for us. She strung eight beads on a white string and hung it across the kitchen window. Each bead represented one of her children. As she would pray for us by name, she would move "our" bead across the window to the other side. She loved her children with such a fervent love and wanted a peaceful, happy life for them. Day after day, she was faithful to pray because she believed in a God *who was faithful to answer.*

As a young girl, my mom had walked down the aisle of her church with her sister, Nancy, and given her life to Jesus. She used to tell us about her God and His love for us, how He wanted to be our Friend and take care of us and love us. Yet, when I was a teenage boy, full of my own ideas about life, none of that talk about God ever got through to me. I figured my mom was just out of touch with reality.

Mom used to tell me how God could do anything, that nothing was impossible for Him. What she said didn't matter to me, except one time when I needed some extra help. I was standing in front of a judge a few months before the accident, facing a possible short jail sentence, and I sure prayed! "God, if You get me out of this jam, I'll get my act together!" Now, that's a prayer prayed by millions of desperate people!

Well, He answered me, and the sentence was suspended. So, I did what most people do...I went right back to my lifestyle. Mom reminded me of my prayer and then prayed for me some more. She had such a confidence about her relationship with God and His ability to perform the impossible.

"WHERE IS THIS GREAT GOD NOW?"

Now, the night of the accident, Mom's faith was severely tested. She listened numbly as the nurses explained I had slipped into a coma and that it would be best if she and my father went home and returned the next morning. On the way home from the hospital, she cried bitterly about her oldest sons' lives. It seemed as if everything they did was wrong! Why did this happen? The drugs, the alcohol, the trouble— when would it stop? Was she to blame? Had she done something wrong? Where was God now?

The enemy of her soul, Satan, also called the devil, who fights against God and His work in this world, was relentless, proclaiming the power he had over her husband and her children. It was as though she could hear him say to her, *Where is this great God now? Where is this power He claims to have? Why do things only seem to get worse for you and your children?* The ugly voice went on, *Now, your son Jim is so bad that you don't know if he will ever see out of his left eye again! You don't know if he has permanent brain damage! His face is so cut up, he'll never look the same. Where is this loving God you claim to serve? Why is this happening to you again and again?*

After my parents arrived back at the house, Mom went to her room and fell on her knees beside her bed. She wanted the voice of the enemy to stop;

> **Mom went to her room and fell on her knees beside her bed. She wanted the voice of the enemy to stop; she wanted to hear the voice of her God.**

she wanted to hear the voice of her God. In the same spot where she had spent so many hours praying for her family, she cried out to the Lord, "God, please don't let Jim be blind. Please, Jesus, touch him."

At first, her fear and sense of despair threatened to stop her prayers. She knew deep in her heart that God could do anything, but the weight on her shoulders just seemed too much to carry. There was that voice of the enemy telling her that even prayer was hopeless this time. She knew that God could not fail at anything, but she wondered how much more she could take. "Help me, Lord," she cried.

I imagine that she was feeling what King David expressed in one of the psalms in the Bible; Jesus Himself quoted the first line when He was on the cross:

> *My God, My God, why have You forsaken Me? Why are You so far from helping Me, and from the words of My groaning? O My God, I cry in the daytime, but You do not hear; and in the night season, and am not silent.* (Psalm 22:1–2)

But, slowly, Mom sensed God's presence fill the room. As she prayed, she felt the weight of her pain and fear being lifted from her shoulders. Suddenly, she found herself in a wonderful state of praise and adoration. Her faith was being renewed by the presence and the power of the Holy Spirit. He is the One who is here with us to be both our Comforter and our Guide. He was renewing Mom's strength and faith as she called out in prayer.

What had happened? What made the difference for her, and what can make the difference for all of us? It's the truth found in the next few verses of Psalm 22:

> But You are holy, enthroned in the praises of Israel. Our fathers trusted in You; they trusted, and You delivered them. They cried to You, and were delivered; they trusted in You, and were not ashamed.   (verses 3–5)

In other words, God was just waiting for her praise, and I can almost see Him pouring out His Holy Spirit on her to equip her to praise Him, because He is enthroned in the praises of His people, or He "inhabits" them, as it says in an earlier Bible translation. The word *"enthroned"* in the original Hebrew means "to sit down and watch," or "to be absorbed with." It is as if God is waiting for the impossible situation that His people truly need Him for, that only God can make right. He just wants our praise and trust, and then He moves in with all of His power, and nothing can compete with His presence.

This is a truth that allows us to transcend all worry; it takes us past unbelief and fear. Praise is a weapon that can bring down spiritual wickedness in high places. Praise is a key component of our victories in life. When we say the words *"But You are holy,"* we introduce the game changer! Those words don't necessarily mean that what we need will show up immediately. They do show that we know God is holy and that, because of that knowledge, we rest assured that He is fighting our battles for us and that we can trust in Him. When we praise God, He is absorbed with us and is so proud of us; He can see all the fear, doubt, and unbelief that Satan has thrown at us, and yet He sees that we will offer the sacrifice of praise to His name, even before we see the actual manifestation of our answered prayers. God is always looking for people who will praise Him in that way, because they trust in Him.

> The spark of hope God placed in her heart began to fan into a larger fire of faith.

And this is what He did for my mom on that terrible night. Suddenly, the spark of hope God placed in her heart began to fan into a larger fire of faith. It was as if the Holy Spirit was proclaiming the promises of God to her. She could see the Bible verses she had read so many times, as though they were on a movie screen:

Behold, I am the LORD, the God of all flesh. Is there anything too hard for Me?
(Jeremiah 32:27)

If you then, being evil, know how to give good gifts to your children, how much more will your Father who is in heaven give good things to those who ask Him!
(Matthew 7:11)

Ask, and it will be given to you; seek, and you will find; knock, and it will be opened to you. For everyone who asks receives, and he who seeks finds, and to him who knocks it will be opened. *(Matthew 7:7–8)*

> *Call upon Me in the day of trouble; I will de-*
> *liver you, and you shall glorify Me.*
>   (Psalm 50:15)

Once again, God had shown up powerfully to encourage my mom. She *would not* give up on Him, on the faithful promises in the Bible, or on me. She began to praise the Lord for who He is and what He had done for her! She wouldn't insult Him with any complaints. She began to worship Him and proclaim His holiness and His power. As she sang His praises, she knew that the Holy Spirit was renewing her faith. The more she praised Him, the stronger she became. Regardless of what she saw in the natural, her God—the almighty God, as she called Him—was in total control of her life and mine!

4

Terrified by Darkness

Darkness surrounded me, and I was falling. I tried to grab something to break the fall, but there was nothing there. Again, I was six feet three inches, a fairly big guy. I was used to working my way out of most situations, but this time I had gone too far. The situation was out of my control.

I was in some strange place. Wherever it was, I knew I was not meant to be there. I knew that the God my mother talked about didn't mean for me to be there, either. Where was I? This place was out of my league...and I was scared!

Two weeks before this, I'd been driving out of the parking lot of the Mister Donut shop in my hometown, and I'd felt God's hand on my left shoulder, tugging on me and telling me to slow down because I was going to kill myself. I just hadn't wanted to hear it, so I'd told Him to get off me and leave me alone; I wanted to live my life my way. I had a couple of joints in my visor, a quart of beer between my legs, and who knows what in the glove box, and I didn't want to hear anything from anybody. Now, I wished I had listened!

The feeling of falling stopped, but I was still in darkness. I turned my head and looked to my left. I could see something like a shadow standing beside me in the near blackness. Slowly, I realized there were two creature-like things looking at me, glaring menacingly. Whatever they were, they seemed to be laughing at me with a very evil presence all around them. At that moment, I realized they *wanted* me; they wanted to *overwhelm me with their power.* And I lay there, helpless to stop them.

> I would have laughed at the very thought of demons if I hadn't seen them myself. What was I going to do?

My whole body tensed with fright. I had never seen demons before, but I had heard about them from my mom many times. They were in league with Satan. I guess I would have laughed at the very thought of them—even today—if I hadn't seen them myself. Now, they were right next to me, and I had to make a decision quickly. What was I going to do?

From the darkness, it was as though I could hear my mom reminding me of the power of prayer. "Jimmy, God is the God of the impossible," she seemed to say. It didn't sound so foolish anymore. But was it too late for me? Up to this point, I had always believed that I could party until I was an old man, maybe eighty. Then, I would admit my sins to God, get everything cleaned up, and slip right into heaven. I never wanted to hear any of the things my mom would say about God. I wanted to live life on my terms until the end…but look where it had led me. I knew in my soul that I was about to get everything I deserved right then. I didn't know this Bible verse at the time, but it described me perfectly:

> *The pangs of death surrounded me, and the floods of ungodliness made me afraid. The sorrows of Sheol surrounded me; the snares of death confronted me. In my distress I called upon the LORD, and cried out to my God; He heard my voice from His temple, and my cry came before Him, even to His ears.…He delivered me from my strong enemy, from those who hated me, for they were too strong for me. They confronted me in the day of my calamity, but the LORD was my support. He also brought me out into a broad place;* ***He delivered me because He delighted in me***.
> (Psalm 18:4–6, 17–19, emphasis added)

Now *that* is the miracle of God's love, mercy, and grace: He delivers us because He delights in us! He loves us when we deserve it the least! That is the definition of His grace. He doesn't give us what we *deserve*. He gives us His grace, His love, His very best— His Son, *Jesus Christ*. In my case, He also gave me a fervent, praying mother. She was at home praying for me on her knees as I was experiencing the most frightening moment of my life.

SURE THAT IT WAS TIME FOR ME TO DIE

To the hospital staff, I was unconscious, lying on that hospital bed as the nurses and doctors monitored my every heartbeat. But inside my mind, I was wide awake and facing two of the ugliest creatures you can imagine. Again, I knew that the black creatures before me were two demons. Years later, God explained to me that those demons were living *in me* at the time. They were the demons of alcohol and drugs. They were standing there because they had come to claim their property. They were sure that it was time for me to die.

At that very moment, when it seemed as though all was lost, *Jesus came to me.* He appeared, and I saw Him! I knew it was Jesus—but, somehow, I can't describe Him. (You know how different things can be in our subconscious minds from things in the physical world.) As Jesus looked at me in my pitiful, injured state, He said to me, "Jim, you've been living your life your own way long enough. Do you want to continue this way?"

I looked back at Him and answered, "Jesus, what do You want me to do? I've tried so many times to get things straight, but I have failed so often. It seems so hopeless. What do I need to do? Become a priest or a monk? Lock myself up in a room and just read the Bible for the rest of my life?"

I knew it was my fault that my life was such a mess. It wasn't Jesus' fault. I was the one to blame. But I didn't understand that it wasn't about what *I* had to do to fix my situation and make myself right with God. It was about what *He* had already done on the cross of Calvary.

When I looked at Jesus in that moment, all I saw was His forgiveness and the overwhelming knowledge that He really cared for me—with compassion and a gentleness that could not be denied. Even though He didn't speak at that moment, I could sense His love for me pouring forth from His heart. He was not going to leave me; He was there to help me in the depths of the prison I had created for myself.

I had never felt such a presence before. When He spoke again, a shower of peace and joy fell upon me. I knew in an instant that Jesus Christ was real and that anything He spoke to me would be true. Even before He spoke, it was as though I could hear His words deep in my heart, soul, and mind.

> I knew in an instant that Jesus Christ was real and that anything He spoke to me would be true.

As Jesus looked at me, He said simply, "Jim, if you ask Me to cleanse you and forgive you, I will. I will never leave you or forsake you. I will give you the power to overcome the drugs and alcohol. I will walk with you and be your Friend."

I was amazed. I knew how I weighed in on the scales of sin and goodness. And yet Jesus had come to help me. He willingly reached out to me in my unworthy state. In His love, He looked past all the ugly, worthless things I'd felt about myself for all those years, and He loved me. His genuine concern for me was beautiful—so real and true that I knew He meant every word He spoke. I hardly knew what to say in response.

Looking into Jesus' loving eyes, I said, "Jesus, please help me; please forgive me. I know I am a sinner. I know I screwed up again, and I know I need

Your help." The moment I spoke those words and asked Jesus to help me, those two demons that were standing beside me vanished! A great peace washed over me. I didn't know what it all meant, but I did know one thing—I had been set free!

> *But you, O Lord, are a compassionate and gracious God, slow to anger, abounding in love and faithfulness. Turn to me and have mercy on me; grant your strength to your servant.* (Psalm 86:15–16 NIV)

> *You have cast all my sins behind Your back.* (Isaiah 38:17)

NEVER BLIND AGAIN

While my mother was at home, on her knees, crying out to God for His help during the most crucial moments of my life, she saw something that gave her great peace. Later, at the hospital, she told me about it: "Jim, when I was praying for you, I was asking God to touch your eyes so you would not be blind. In my prayers, I saw the hand of God reach down, and, with His index finger, He touched your left eye. When I saw this, I knew God had healed you and that you would not lose your eyesight. At that moment, I knew you would be well."

Little did she know, at that very moment, Jesus had made things right in *every* part of my life. I would never be blind again. My spiritual eyes were finally going to be truly opened.

As I wrote earlier, while I was seeing the vision of Jesus, I was lying on the operating table.

The operating team pulled more glass from my eyes and face; and, for over six hours, the plastic surgeon worked on me. I needed over three hundred stitches in my face and head just to begin the process of sewing me back together. At the same time, they operated on my jaw. My jaw bone was broken, so they had to repair it and wire my mouth shut. Those wires would hold my jaw together for the next six weeks.

After the surgery, I was in a coma for several days. My sister Jane worked with our next-door neighbor, Pat, as a candy striper at the hospital. When she arrived at the hospital the day after the accident and saw Pat, she asked, "Did you see Jim?" Pat said no and wondered what Jane was talking about. She said, "The only man here is in the room down the hall." When Jane said, "That has to be him," Pat looked at her with an expression that said, *I hope that is not Jim.* Jane walked into the room and saw me lying completely still and wrapped like a mummy. She felt totally numb as she looked at me. The gauze bandages that covered my head had dried blood on them. The medical staff had left only a tiny opening in the bandages for my mouth in order for a tube to be placed into it, and two tiny openings in each nostril, with tubes in them, as well. "It was horrendous. I was just overwhelmed completely," Jane told me later.

> I was lying completely still, my body wrapped like a mummy. The bandages covering my head had dried blood on them, and there were only tiny openings for my mouth and nose.

When I finally regained consciousness in intensive care, I grabbed the sheets on my bed because I didn't know where I was. My head was still wrapped, with all the gauze protecting the stitches in my face and head. A nurse was standing nearby and looking at me with concern. She told me that her name was Toni, but then I passed out again. I woke up long enough to see that they had moved me to another room. I guess that since I was no longer in a coma, I didn't have to be in intensive care any longer.

The next time I woke up, my mom and dad were standing beside my bed. I could not see or really talk to anyone because the bandages covered my entire head, including my face, and my jaw was wired shut. Just the same, I *had* to tell my mother what had happened to me while I was in surgery. The first words I tried to mutter through my broken jaw shocked my parents: "Mom, Jesus is here! Jesus is here!"

My sweet mother told me later that she looked down at me in amazement, her eyes filling with tears. God had not only spared me, but a miracle was also happening! It was truly the answer to her prayers. She had known from the night of the accident when she'd cried out to the Lord that He had heard her.

There I was, with dried blood all over my face and head. Five tubes in my body feeding and draining me. And a long road of extensive plastic surgery lying ahead of me. Yet, somehow, in all of this, my mom was at peace. She had broken through that night and walked into the presence of God in prayer. She learned once again that nothing was impossible for the God she served. This was the God I was soon going to learn so much about.

5

OVER THREE HUNDRED STITCHES

For the next couple of weeks, I lay in my hospital bed wondering what had happened to me during that surgery. I should have been afraid, but I had an amazing peace deep inside. One morning, the doctors walked into my hospital room and told me they would take off the bandages in the next few days. "I'm afraid you should expect the worst, Jim," one doctor warned. "Remember, we had to put over three hundred stitches in your face and head."

Strangely, all the time I was listening to him, I was still filled with peace about everything. The damage to my face, the question of my eyesight— none of that seemed to matter. The doctors were waiting for an emotional reaction, for fear or anger, but I couldn't explain the peace in my soul. I couldn't really say much at all with my jaw wired shut! So, I just assured them that I was okay.

When my younger brother, Bill, came in to see me, it was pretty much the same. First, he stuck his head in the room, but when he looked at me with all the bandages, wrapped like a mummy, he left because he thought he had the wrong room. When he went to the nurses' station and found out it was the right room, he was pretty shaken up. Bill and I were close in age and close as brothers, in spite of our having the typical fights. When I looked at Bill's face, it finally dawned on me how serious the accident was to everyone—my facial damage, the glass in my eyes, the possible damage to my brain. Yet the peace still never left me. All I could say to Bill was that I really was going to be all right.

Early one morning, the doctors walked into my room, ready to take the bandages off. They had asked my parents to be there for support when I got my first look at my damaged face. I remember looking at their anxious expressions; they were so certain that I was going to have a terrible reaction to my injuries. What they didn't understand was how thankful I was just to be alive. The fact that God had given me a second chance had become so real to me that I knew I could deal with whatever came next.

"MAN, ARE YOU UGLY!"

The doctor began to gently unwrap the thin white gauze from my face and head. The gauze stuck to the stitches and the dried blood, so it was a very slow process. Once he removed the final wrapping, he just sat quietly on the bed next to me and slowly examined my cuts one by one, wiping them down with alcohol to clean my face up the best he could.

Looking me in the eye, the doctor reminded me of how my face would appear with the thread sticking out of the three hundred stitches, and then he handed me a small mirror.

I sat there for a moment and stared into the mirror with dozens of thoughts racing through my mind. How should I react to this? Was I supposed to be upset?

My face looked like a railroad depot because there were so many stitches all over the place. The stitches all around my eyes and forehead seemed to run together. My face was swollen from the cuts. You could see just where the windshield had dug into my right cheekbone when I was dragged back into the car. There was a long cut that went across my nose and down to my lower lip, and it made my mouth look distorted. You could tell the intern had done the best he could, but he was not a plastic surgeon. The right side of my chin was probably the worst, due to the compound fracture. The entire right side of my face was pulled down because of the number of stitches in that area that ran down over my chin.

> I stared into the mirror with dozens of thoughts racing through my mind. My face looked like a railroad depot. But I was so grateful to be alive that I couldn't be upset.

My dad tried to lighten the atmosphere by quipping, "Man, are you ugly!" He always liked to control the moment by saying something funny, and he just wanted to help me through this. Everyone was waiting for me to speak, watching for my reaction to all the thread in my face.

I looked carefully at every part of my face; what could I say? I was just so grateful to be alive that I couldn't be upset. Although I could not explain to anyone just how important Jesus' visit had been to me when I was unconscious, it was okay. I knew I was the one who had caused this mess, and, at the same time, I knew I was forgiven. Somehow, everything was going to be all right.

While I lay in that hospital bed, all I could think of was how Jesus had come to me and how the demons had fled. I was so thankful to the God of the universe for giving me another chance at life!

"You've Hit Your Head a Little Too Hard, Buddy"

If you had asked me any religious questions, such as "Are you born again?" or "Have you been saved?" I honestly would not have known what you were talking about. I had never read the Bible; I had never been to any kind of prayer meeting or any meeting where Jesus had been the main topic of discussion. Remember, up until now, my concept of Christianity was to party as hard as I could and then get things cleaned up with God. The closest I'd ever gotten to a Bible was to see one on a shelf somewhere. Now, as I lay there with tubes feeding me and draining me, I couldn't help but wonder how my life was about to change.

I didn't think about what to tell my buddies until they came in to see me a few days later. They brought some wine and told me they would bring in some drugs if I wanted some "relief." I remember telling them I didn't need those things anymore, that I had met God and I would be fine.

First, they looked at each other, and then they looked down at me. "You've hit your head a little too hard, buddy," one of them chirped up. "You'll be okay in a little while!" I didn't know how else to explain what had happened to me. They just shook their heads, and we talked about other things.

This deep peace I had for the first time in my life seemed to override every emotion that started rising up within me. The peace remained whenever I thought about my face, what I was going to do next, how I was going to hang out with my friends—and what I was going to do about the Marines.

What About the Marines?

Again, this was 1971. The United States had been involved in the war in Vietnam since the early 1960s. I had enlisted in the Marine Corps just a few weeks before the accident. That's another reason I had been partying so hard. I wanted to have as much fun as I could because I thought I would be going to Vietnam. My oldest brother, Jack, had just come home from Vietnam, and from everything he had described, I knew it was no party over there, so I had better have my fun now!

I was brought up to believe I had an obligation to serve my country. From the time I was ten years old, I knew I would become a marine. Whatever I had to do to become a good marine, I was willing to pay the price because I had been raised to love America. At eighteen years of age, I was totally ignorant of the grave situation in Southeast Asia. I just wanted to stand up for America and do my part. I knew I could do that, and what better place than in the United States Marines?

The Marine recruiter came in to the hospital to see me as soon as I was conscious. He was very concerned and told us that I could be released from my enlistment because of the physical damage I had suffered. I thought about it for half a second, but I knew that becoming a marine was not just something I wanted to do; it was something I *had* to do. Besides all that, I realized now that I needed to get away from my buddies and the drug scene that had become so important to me. I needed a break from it all, and the U.S. Marines and Vietnam seemed to be where I was headed.

6

LEAVING THE HOSPITAL

After I had been in the hospital for more than two weeks, I was told I was going to be discharged the next day, but my dad came in around ten o'clock the night before and told me to get my stuff. "We're leaving now," he said gruffly. I told him I had to check out in the morning, but he just repeated that we were leaving right then. Remember, Big Jack was six feet four inches and two hundred eighty-five pounds. He'd had a few drinks, and you just didn't argue with him. So, I got all my things together, and we left.

My dad was a great guy, and I really loved him, but how I hated to see him drunk! When booze was not involved, he was awesome. He was a man's man, and I'd been so proud of him as a young kid. But as I'd grown older and seen how the alcohol destroyed him and my family, how it hurt my mom, I'd sworn I would never be like him. The truth was, I ended up loving the booze as much as he did, and getting wasted became my favorite thing.

So, as we drove home from the hospital that night, I had many conflicting thoughts. I knew I could never stay sober by myself; I needed Jesus to take all this conflict away and help me start my life again. Little did I realize I *had* started my life again the *moment* I'd asked Jesus to forgive me while I was lying on that operating table. At that very moment, I'd been born again.

On our way home, we passed the country club where the party had been the night of the accident. Our house was close by, so we usually made a right turn there and drove up Long Road to our home. This time, I told my dad to keep driving straight up the road and to our family church.

"Why do you want to go there? It's late, and it will be closed. No one will be there now," he countered. Through my broken and wired jaw, I muttered again, "Please, Dad, just take me there now."

He realized I was serious and drove straight to the church. When we pulled into the parking lot, I told him to stay there and I would be right out. Back then, they left the churches open at night. I pulled on the heavy wooden door and walked inside the dark sanctuary. I made my way slowly down front to the altar and got on my knees. I looked up at the cross with the soft light shining from the outside window, and I told Jesus Christ how grateful I was to Him for coming to me and thanked Him for giving me a second chance. I told Him I knew what He'd done for me when I was unconscious and how He had stood up for me against those two creatures. I knew He'd given me His love and forgiveness. I knew He'd promised that He would never leave me or forsake me. But I told Him I had no idea what to do next. I didn't know what my life would become or how to go about daily living because everything was different inside me. I really needed His help to figure all this out.

I couldn't blame my friends for doing drugs and getting in trouble because, a few weeks earlier, I had been right with them. I knew I wasn't going to do those things anymore, but where was I going to go? Who would I hang out with? How would I spend my time? What did God expect of me now?

> How could I explain what I had seen while I was unconscious? How could I tell my friends that Jesus had set me free, and that He loved me and them?

Again, I had never read the Bible, so I had no idea how God intervened in a life. And what was I to do with the news of how Jesus had come to me? How could I explain to anyone besides my mom what I had seen while I was unconscious? How could I find the words to tell my friends that Jesus had set me free, and that He loved me and them? Would they understand that He really wanted me to be His friend and wanted to be my Friend?

That night in the darkened church, I just prayed and asked God to help me with all of these overwhelming questions. It was way too much for me to handle, and I knew I couldn't do it by myself. But I figured that since He had freed me from the dark place with those horrible demons, there was nothing He couldn't handle. Feeling His peace again, I got up from the altar and walked back outside to meet my dad.

Facing Family and Friends

After the stop at the church, we drove to our house. When we pulled into the driveway, I knew my mom was waiting to see me; she just wanted me home. Most of my family members were there, and I saw the look in their eyes when they caught sight of my face. The surgical team had had to shave off a lot of my hair, the scars were still very red, the cut on my head was very large, and I wasn't able to shave my face. My face was also still swollen from the accident, the surgery, and the removal of many of the stitches. The doctor hadn't been able to take out all of the stitches in one sitting because there were so many of them, so I still had some stitches left in my face!

Sure, the obvious thing to say to me was, "You really screwed up this time, Jim! Now what are you going to do?" Instead of saying that, my family just loved me. We had a lot of dysfunction, like most families. Our family life was very tough because of how alcohol dominated our existence. But if we did anything right, it was to rally around each other during hard times. We tried to be there for each other in spite of the difficulties. When the chips were down, I always knew my seven brothers and sisters would be there for me. They all broke down and cried and had to leave the room after they saw me because they thought I would never look the same. But because of their support, I don't have a single picture of my face after the accident. They didn't want me to remember how bad it looked.

Back to the Red Flame

Since I didn't know what to do next, I just took a few weeks to heal up. Then, with the scars on my face a constant reminder of what had happened to me, I headed right back to a favorite bar, the Red Flame, to meet my friends. After all, I couldn't stay home forever, and where else was I going to go?

Everyone greeted me with shouts and back slaps, and then we got into a buddy's car and just started driving around. The usual took place: someone lit a joint, and someone else cracked open the booze. They all were very cool with me and felt bad about what had happened; they wanted me to get high and have a good time and forget about all the pain.

They meant no harm, and if it were not for my experience with Jesus, I would have been the one ready to start the party. When the joint was handed to me, I told them I didn't want it and just passed it over to the next guy.

"Whoa, what's up with you?" my friends asked. "I really don't need it anymore," I answered simply. That started a lot of questions. I was very nervous and uncertain of what to say. I wanted to tell them how God had touched me and helped me, how His presence and my prayer had chased the demons away. I wanted to describe the peace I had in the hospital and when I prayed to Jesus in the church on the way home. But, truthfully, I didn't want them to think I was weird now.

I knew what we thought about those fanatic religious folks. "Born-again weirdos," "Hare Krishna chanters"—they were all the same to us: losers, freaks, selling flowers in the airports! What was I going to say? I didn't know any Scriptures yet. As I sat there wondering what to do, smoke filled the entire car, and everyone was beginning to feel pretty high. I had to say something; I wasn't drinking or smoking the joint or taking a hit off the pipe. Everyone wanted to hear something from me *right now*. And, with the wires still in my jaw, I couldn't even talk clearly.

All I remember telling them that night was that God had given me another chance, and I wasn't going back. I told them I had screwed up enough, and I had asked God to help me. They knew about my life during the past six months: almost going to jail, being chased by cops, getting into fights, having the accident, my face.

They were pretty cool with it all. Someone said, laughingly, "You'll be all right, Jim; it will just take a while for you to get back to normal." Then, one of my closest buddies said, "Come on, man, leave him alone; he's been through enough." That ended the conversation about me for that night. But I knew it was really only the beginning. It might take me a little while, but I had so much to say, and I would have to find some way to say it.

> I, Jim Maxim, had really turned down the drugs and booze. Man, I *was* different. I think I shocked myself.

When we got back to the bar, I headed home and started thinking about what had just happened. I had really turned down the drugs, and I hadn't had any booze. I, Jim Maxim, had just told a group of guys how *God* had touched me. Man, I *was* different. I think I shocked myself.

I knew I couldn't keep up with that scene; instead, it was

time to focus on the Marines. It was good for me to be leaving town. I was scheduled to leave in about sixty days, and I needed to be as ready as I could be. So I started working out harder, running a lot, and getting ready for Parris Island, South Carolina, and Marine Corps boot camp.

7

THE FEW...THE PROUD...

My dad dropped me off at the bus station in downtown Pittsburgh for the trip to the airport. He was happy I was going because he knew I needed to get away from the old environment. My wanting to serve my country made Big Jack very proud. He didn't understand spiritual matters, but he knew that somehow things were better with me.

You wouldn't think your life could change just waiting for a bus, but mine did that day. I found a little New Testament and Psalms Bible sitting on a small table beside my chair. The Gideons, a group of Christian businessmen, had placed several of them around the terminal. I guess the bus station was known as a place for people in need!

I still had not read the Bible and had no clue what was really in there. I picked up this copy, opened to the first few introductory pages, and read something like this: "When in trouble, turn to page 100," or "When needing guidance, turn to page 200." The one that I remember most clearly said, "When leaving home or feeling lonely, turn to page ___."

> As I started reading the Bible, I wanted to somehow eat the pages and get them deep inside of me where I would never lose them.

As I started reading from the Bible, it was as if water from a fire hose was being pumped deep into my heart. The words were jumping off the pages of this little book! I couldn't read it fast enough, and I wanted to somehow eat the pages and get them deep inside of me where I would never lose them or forget them. With every page, I was receiving strength and comfort. Even though the words were new to me, they all seemed to make such sense. Words like, *"I will never leave you nor forsake you"* (Hebrews 13:5), and *"He shall call upon Me, and I will answer him"* (Psalm 91:15), and *"Christ Jesus came into the world to save sinners"* (1 Timothy 1:15).

The Bible verse that shook my soul was, *"Behold, I stand at the door and knock. If anyone hears My voice and opens the door, I will come in to him and dine with him, and he with Me"* (Revelation 3:20). It was a personal invitation from Jesus.

This was the same Jesus who had come to me when I was unconscious, and now I was watching Him come to the people in the New Testament, touching them, healing them, loving them. He was reaching out to the "down-and-outers," the poor, the oppressed, and the needy. He was hanging out with sinners, just being their Friend. He was identifying with the people who needed His help the most, just as He'd done with me.

I walked onto the bus and sat down, still reading page after page. I found a verse that said, *"For the Son of Man has come to seek and to save that which was lost"* (Luke 19:10). Another Scripture said that Jesus didn't come for the healthy people but for the sick and needy! (See Mark 2:17.) This book had real power attached to it! I grabbed it tightly and pressed it against my chest, just wanting to get the words inside of me. For the first time in my life, I realized I had a road map to turn to for guidance. The answers to my questions were in this book!

I couldn't believe it. I was being overpowered with the same presence that had been with me when I was unconscious. It was like it was happening all over again. Why had I never read this book before?

Even today, when I share Jesus with others and they want to argue with me or tell me I'm naïve, I ask them if they have ever read the Bible. Most people say no, but they think they know what's in it. How foolish to reject something if you have never read it. They don't understand that the Bible contains words that are alive and have the power to bring life-saving changes to the people who read them with faith.

PARRIS ISLAND

We arrived in South Carolina and were met by a couple of Marine Corps sergeants waiting for recruits coming from all over the country. We gave them our names and boarded a bus to Parris Island. It was after midnight, and the drive from the airport was through the deep woods and then the swamps of South Carolina. What was this place going to be like?

We drove through the gates and stopped. A drill instructor boarded the bus and said something to the bus driver. I saw the driver just put his head down, and then...*it started.* The drill instructor began screaming everything you can imagine to move us quickly off that bus. The first thing he screamed was, "You had better give your soul to God because your ___ is mine!" It wasn't the reference to God I would have hoped for!

> Suddenly, there were five screaming drill instructors trying their best to intimidate us and let us know that, for the next fourteen weeks, we belonged to them.

Suddenly, there were five screaming drill instructors trying their best to intimidate us and let us know that, for the next fourteen weeks, we belonged to them. As we walked into the first building to begin our transformation from life as civilians to life in the Marines, we passed under a sign that read, "Through this portal pass prospects for the world's finest fighting force, *the United States Marines.*" I wondered why the word *prospects* was written there; didn't everyone who walked under that sign become a marine? The next morning, I would start to find out why.

It was 5:00 a.m. I thought I had just closed my eyes, but the drill instructors were yelling at us to get out of bed and get downstairs. I never saw so many guys move so fast in all my life; nobody wanted to be the last one down the steps.

They lined us up on both sides of a table with small dividers on top of it. We were commanded to empty our pockets and place everything in the space right in front of us. Brass knuckles, knives, and every other thing imaginable were emptied out of those pockets. Obviously, these drill instructors knew what they were looking for!

As they continued shouting out orders, one big guy was just acting tough. The drill instructor called him over, and the guy moved toward him with a hardguy kind of swagger. That drill instructor grabbed the recruit's Adam's apple and jacked him up against one of the pillars in the squad bay until his legs were off the ground. He was kicking and gasping for air, while the sergeant endlessly screamed at him, telling him he was a "useless maggot" and a "waste of human flesh." Finally, he pushed the big guy across the room and told him to get back in line.

You could have heard a pin drop in that room. No one dared breathe a word or move a muscle. Those drill instructors were hardened combat veterans, and they were not going to allow any punk prospect to become a marine or to wear the uniform of the U.S. Marines—a uniform that so many other men had paid the ultimate price to wear while defending their country—if he was not the right type of man.

I used to think my brother Jack had exaggerated about Parris Island and what the drill instructors were like, but after this "Welcome to 'Our Island'" speech, I decided I would go along with the program for the next fourteen weeks and do what I was told, when I was told—no questions asked!

8

"The Private Just Believes in God, Sir"

Every chance I got, I opened that little Bible from the bus station. I would turn to the book of Psalms and read something like this:

> *But You, O Lord, are a shield for me, my glory and the One who lifts up my head. I cried to the Lord with my voice, and He heard me from His holy hill. I lay down and slept; I awoke, for the Lord sustained me. I will not be afraid of ten thousands of people who have set themselves against me all around.* (Psalm 3:3–6)

Whenever I needed strength to get through my day, I would just open that little book, and the words seemed to jump off the pages and into my heart. One drill instructor asked me why I carried that little Bible in my pocket.

"Are you a preacher, Maxim?" he asked. "No, sir," I answered, "the private just believes in God, sir." The sergeant would look at my scarred face and begin his tirades: "Maxim, it looks like you went to a hatchet fight and left your hatchet at home!" "It looks like you to tried to French kiss a freight train," and on and on.

None of that ever bothered me; it was just a reminder of what happened to me when I saw Jesus. My scarred face also gave me many opportunities to talk about my newfound faith. Naturally, most of the guys would ask me what had happened. Their questions opened the door for me to tell them about the wreck and what my lifestyle had been like at the time. Most of them identified with me right away. We could have been friends at the Christmas party that night. When they heard I had passed out behind the wheel, they asked a million questions, such as "Did you hit the other guy?" and "Were you tripping at the time?" and "How did they ever get you fixed up with all that bleeding?"

All of their questions made my faith in Jesus Christ that much more real as I told them how I had been in big trouble and God got me out of the jam. Then, I related all of the details of when Jesus appeared to me while I was on the operating table. It all made perfect sense to them. When they saw me reading the Bible, and then looked at my face, they remembered what had happened when I was unconscious. They accepted my story; to them, it seemed so real. We had become friends, and they trusted what I had to say. They knew I was sincere in my story.

Even today, when I talk of my love for Jesus Christ, I look forward to just being someone's friend, to being real with him. I can't shove the Bible down anyone's throat, so why try? Jesus came to me because He loved me and He wanted to help me. He wanted me to know that He loved me enough to show up in my life when I needed Him the most. Jesus is always looking to help someone. When people see and feel that you are being genuine with them, and that you really want to understand where they are in their lives, then Jesus becomes real to them, too.

> When people see that you are being genuine with them, and that you really want to understand where they are in their lives, then Jesus becomes real to them, too.

The fourteen weeks of boot camp were some of the hardest days of my life. No marine could ever forget them, and yet the experience of boot camp is something he will treasure for life. That rite of passage, the privilege of putting on that uniform, carries a certain dignity and pride that this nation has admired for more than two hundred twenty-five years, and its enemies have feared. And I had the privilege of getting through those days with the help of my new-found faith. Now, it was time to move on.

Saving Face...Literally!

While I was in the Marines, God wanted to show me how much He cared about the details of my life. Even today, as I think about those Marine Corps days, I remain amazed at His love.

After Parris Island, I was stationed at Camp Lejeune in North Carolina. My face was strangely disproportioned because of the inexperience of the intern who had sewed me up. I had lumps of skin on my face and chin. Where my jaw had been broken, I was left with a very wide scar, and the place where my nose had first hit the windshield was just rough skin. And, again, the jagged glass had left a scar that started under my right eye and ran straight down my face. I still never thought much about it until someone started staring at me or asked me what had happened.

One day, my captain came to me and ordered, "Maxim, go down to the hospital and get your face fixed!" I said, "Yes, sir," went over to the hospital, walked to the front desk, and asked, "Who should I see to get my face fixed?"

The hospital personnel told me that a plastic surgeon traveled there from the Naval Hospital in Portsmouth, Virginia, once a month, and I should check back then. This was because a lot of the guys who came back from Vietnam had been wounded and needed plastic surgery, so different surgeons would come monthly to take care of them.

I returned later that month and told the surgeon that my captain wanted me to get my face fixed. His response was, "Sorry, son, we don't do cosmetic surgery on marines." I said, "Fine," and then I left. But my captain wasn't content with that answer. He told me that, the following month, I had to go back to talk to the surgeon again. The next surgeon gave me the same response the following month, and again I said, "Fine," and then I left.

When I returned to my captain and explained the answer to him once more, he determinedly responded the same way: "Go back again next month." This was becoming funny to me. I was also learning a valuable lesson that would benefit me for the rest of my life: Persistence always pays off in everything you do.

Month number three came, and I went back. This time, the surgeon from Portsmouth was a "full bird" colonel (a full colonel rather than a lieutenant colonel, as the others had been), and he asked me why I was there. At this point, I was beginning to have fun with this because I knew what was going to come out of his mouth! So, I repeated what I had said the last two times I'd been there. "My captain told me to come down and get my face fixed, sir." I looked intently into his eyes, waiting for the reply I thought would come. Sure enough, he looked at me with a puzzled expression and then told me they do not do cosmetic surgery on marines. I almost started to laugh as I answered, "Fine, sir," and then I began to walk toward the door.

I had gotten a few steps away when, suddenly, he said, "Stop. Have a seat for a minute, son." He started examining my face carefully while asking me what had happened. I explained how I had gone through the windshield and then was pulled back through the broken glass again. "This is pretty bad," he replied as he kept poking and prodding my skin. He had a strange look on his face, and I realized that he wanted to help.

The next words that came out of his mouth floored me. "I'm

> "This is pretty bad," the surgeon said as he poked and prodded my skin. He had a strange look on his face, and I realized he wanted to help.

going to send you to Portsmouth, son. I think I can fix your face." I stared at him in amazement. The Marines were really going to fix me up! I was so very thankful.

The faithfulness of God can be overwhelming! He had stepped in to help me once again. What a reminder that *He* was in control of my life, not the U.S. Army, not the Navy, not even the Marines. To this day, I have not forgotten what He taught me that day so long ago. When something is His will for your life, and you stay open and humble, there is not a door that can stay closed for you. You are His child, and He wants to take care of you.

When I got back to my unit, my captain asked me what the surgeon had said. "They're going to fix me up, sir," I answered with a broad smile. He stood up with an answering grin and shook my hand vigorously. I don't know if my captain was a Christian or not, but, again, he taught me a lesson in persistence that I have always remembered.

In a matter of days, I was transferred to Portsmouth, Virginia, specifically for the surgery. Due to the extent of the damage, I had to have multiple surgeries over six months. When it was done, I had my old face back. The surgical teams recut the scars and removed the scar tissue and then sowed the cuts closer with a finer thread. They performed dermabrasion, sanding my forehead and the side of my eye to remove the lumps and smooth the skin. They cut off and then smoothed over a lump of skin to the side of my mouth. They did Z-plasty surgery on the deepest scar, which was under my right eye. In this procedure, they basically recut the scar, removed the scar tissue, and then pulled the skin upward in the form of a Z so that it was stretched up and out to come almost level to the surface. They also spent a great deal of time trying to narrow the widest scar, which was where my jaw had broken through the skin with the compound fracture. In the end, some lighter scars still remained, but that was okay. These scars served to remind me of the great change Jesus had made in my life when He released me from the captivity of sin. God had used my captain and the surgical teams to give me one of the greatest blessings of my life!

LEARNING TO TRUST GOD

By this time, it was 1973. The Paris Peace Accords were signed between the United States, North Vietnam, South Vietnam, and the Viet Cong. U.S. troops began their withdrawal from South Vietnam, and many POWs were finally sent home. As a result, I never had to go to Vietnam. I served the remainder of my enlistment in Portsmouth as security with the military police. A year later, in March 1974, my service with the United States Marine Corps was completed. I received an honorable discharge and headed back home.

9

STARTING EVERYTHING NEW

Everything had changed. My time away from home and the old environment, and the times I'd spent alone reading God's Word, had altered my life forever. My face had been repaired; my soul had been fixed; my mind had begun to be renewed. The past two years of my life had given me the foundation of a great new beginning. Now, I was on my way home to start everything new.

The time I'd spent in the Marines was important because that was where I learned how to trust God as a young Christian. Knowing and studying God's Word and spending time with Him were vitally important to me then, as they are now. God taught me many personal lessons, even though I never had anyone teach me the Bible while I was a marine. Still, He made sure I was walking close to Him.

There were times during those two years when I did not live like a Christian, but Jesus quickly brought me back to Himself. I asked for forgiveness, and He gave it to me. I found some new Scriptures, such as *"'Come now, and let us reason together,' says the LORD. 'Though your sins are like scarlet, they shall be as white as snow'"* (Isaiah 1:18). God showed me what a loving Father He is and never let me walk out of His protective hand, even when my heart may have wanted something else.

If you have never asked Jesus into your life, or if you are a Christian who has done some things you regret, God is waiting right now with open arms and just asking you to come home. If you call on Him and ask Him to forgive you, He will pick you up in His arms, wash you with the blood of Christ, and make everything (yes, everything!) brand-new once again.

That's the kind of loving heavenly Father you have. God Himself loves to love you. Give Him that chance.

BEGINNING AGAIN, AS A CIVILIAN

At the time I was discharged from the Marine Corps, the country was debating the case of the war in Vietnam, even as it was ending. Public disapproval of the war, or "conflict," as it was known then, was extremely high. The fact that you were a veteran, whether you'd actually fought in Vietnam or not, did not bring the respect that the veterans of our prior wars had received. At that point, our nation didn't know how to distinguish between the politicians and the men and women who were giving their lives for our country, as we do now. It took many years for our nation to get over the Vietnam War and to offer the thanks to our veterans that they deserved. Therefore, when many of the people who were against the war saw a man in uniform, very often, they would say negative things to him, in contrast to the appreciation we see expressed by many people today whenever they see our military men and women in uniform at an airport or in another public place. It was almost as if everyone wanted to just forget about what had happened in Southeast Asia, other than to protest about it. Whenever the subject of Vietnam came up, people usually used slogans, like "baby killers," or mentioned the antiwar protests that had occurred at Kent State University a few years earlier, in 1970, during which four students had been killed by Ohio National Guardsmen. It was a difficult time in our country, because we were thinking our way through the questions of just what our role as the most powerful nation on earth was and what our response should be when other nations call on us for help, as South Vietnam had.

I came home in the midst of this atmosphere, and although it affected me somewhat, I had enough challenges just figuring out what I was going to do with my life and how I was going to live it. I still was figuring out how a person who claimed to believe in Jesus Christ should be living his life, and I really didn't know what to expect or where to begin. I knew I was different spiritually, not just older or more mature, and I was off drugs and alcohol. I truly was a new creation in Christ Jesus, but what did that really mean for me?

> I still was figuring out how a person who claimed to believe in Jesus Christ should be living his life, and I really didn't know where to begin.

This dilemma was especially difficult for me now that there was no set structure to my life, as there had been in the Marines Corps. In the Marines, many of the daily decisions I'd had to make were based upon a certain set of standards, and now those standards were gone. The habits I'd had before I left home and the patterns of my old life had been so centered around alcohol that it was natural for me to remember how I used to live.

REFLECTING ON THE PAST AND NEWNESS OF LIFE

I remember going to the place where I'd had the accident and just walking around the area and reflecting on what had happened, what it all meant, and how it had changed me forever. I would drive by the bars I used to drink in, and the locations where we had picked up the drugs, and the places where we had partied. It really was a unique thing to me, and, during this time, I often would wonder what I would do with my life now that I was home among the places that had bound me in such darkness and yet had this new life inside of me. I asked myself, *Where will I work? How will I spend my time? Who will still be my friends, and where will I find new friends?*

It was also rather surreal at times whenever I met an old friend I used to get high with. The conversations would begin something like, "Hey, Max, do you remember when _____?" and then the memory would return, and the old feeling of being so driven by alcohol would come on me again. Then, instantly, I would think about the accident or falling into that darkness, or about all the pain, injury, and stitches my old lifestyle had given to me. Or, maybe I would think about the time I asked my dad to wait in the car on the way home from the hospital, when I walked into the church and got on my knees at the altar. Or, I might remember something that I had read in the Bible, so I could share it with this person I was talking to. There were times when I would just sit in my car after meeting someone like that and shake my head, thinking about how different I was and about the truth I had been shown by the Lord.

Yes, my life was all very new to me, and yet, at least where the memories were concerned, some of it was very old and familiar, and I knew there was no way I was going back to the old lifestyle. I just didn't know what a lifestyle looked like for a young Christian man. At that time, I still had not seen what Christianity looked like as it was lived out in the real world.

Yet, because of what I had experienced during the past two years, seeing God at work in my life in some very real ways, I figured that He had it all worked out. I just needed to put one foot in front of the other and keep trusting Him to open the doors He had for me. Reflecting on that time now, I see that God had His hand on me, and in every tough situation, the fact that I had been reading the Bible while I was in the Marines gave me the strength I needed to stay focused on Christ.

> God had His hand on me, and in every tough situation, the fact that I had been reading the Bible gave me the strength I needed to stay focused on Christ.

And the adventure was about to get exciting....

A CRUCIAL INTERSECTION

I started school at the University of Pittsburgh, or Pitt, and I began to get back into life as a civilian. Since I had been home only a short while and didn't know where else to meet people, I had started going back to the clubs I used to go to. I had also started dating again, and the girls I met at the clubs and some of the old acquaintances I was spending time with weren't the best for me. I knew I needed some definite direction but didn't know where to find it.

One day, at a fitness club, I ran into a guy named Rick I used to know but had never gotten along with. When I saw him, I remembered my negative opinion of him, and there was a huge conflict going on inside me about how I should treat him. It had been about three years since I had seen him, and so many changes had taken place inside me during that time. We started talking, and, thankfully, nothing from the past seemed to matter. We hit it off and started talking about what was going on in our lives now.

It wasn't long before Rick started telling me about his faith in God. I was a little taken aback because, at this time, I had not met too many outspoken Christians who seemed genuine, had their lives together, and appeared to be people I would want to listen to. He invited me to attend a Bible study with a lot of other college-age people, and it sounded like a good idea.

God was so faithful to me to get me out of the club scene by directing me to this guy who encouraged me to come to the Bible study and meet some like-minded people. I had arrived at a critical intersection at this point in my life. I had to learn what living like a Christian really meant, and I was about to start the process of living out my faith in God the right way.

When I first went to the Bible study, I saw a lot of people my age who were singing and clapping their hands; some even had their hands raised. Even though some of it seemed a little weird and I was uncomfortable, there was also something real about all of them. I saw that they really loved Jesus, and that was an awesome thing for me to witness, even though I had never seen people express their love to Him quite like this. I had met a small group of people when I was at Portsmouth Naval Hospital who had played some Christian songs on a guitar and were very nice. Yet the biggest difference between these new folks and those at the hospital was that they studied the Bible so much. It seemed as if every word out of their mouths was some type of reference to the Bible. I didn't really mind hearing it; I just wondered how somebody could seem to be able to quote all those verses. I mean, I claimed to love Jesus and believe in God, but I didn't know the Bible like they did, and I wasn't even sure at that point if I wanted to be like them.

Sure, I was vocal about my faith, and I loved God and thanked Him daily and even hourly for what He had done for me, but how far was I supposed to go with this?

I had no idea at the time how much pride I had, how I viewed myself, and how I wanted to keep a certain image for myself. I did not know anything about becoming a disciple of Christ. Did I want to become like these people? Was this getting a little like a cult, or what? I still wanted to be around people like those I used to know, even if I didn't want to do what I used to do, and what many of them were still doing. God had been preparing me to start to walk the life of a follower of Jesus, and not just talk the life of a follower. He wanted me to become a disciple of the cross and not just a believer in it.

What did *I* want at the time? I wanted a real good-looking woman, but the club scene was not the place where *He* wanted me to find one. God had different ideas for me, and that knowledge slowly started to sink in.

THE GIFT OF CATHY

I met some good guys at this Bible study, and we started hanging around together at Pitt and at some Christian events. I started growing in my faith and learning more about living in a "Christian community." I don't mean hiding behind a wall or anything, but just becoming a part of the lives of other believers who wanted to make a difference in the world for Christ and wanted to help other people.

But my focus was still on finding a good-looking woman, and I wasn't sure how much God really wanted to help me with this goal. Maybe He knew me a little better than I was willing to admit (an understatement!), and perhaps all my motivations were not as pure as they needed to be, but I was learning that He truly is God. He really does know what is best for me and what will put me in the right position to ultimately serve Him and be as productive for the kingdom of heaven as I can be. Yet, at this stage of my life, I really didn't or couldn't see the big picture of how all that fits together.

One of my friends was telling me about a girl he knew named Cathy whom I should meet and that she was really cool and loved the Lord. I was looking forward to meeting her, and, one day, I was at the church she attended, and she introduced herself to me. Cathy asked me if I remembered her brother Mike, and I did. She said he was in the Navy and was having some problems with drugs and alcohol. She had heard from our mutual friend about how God had touched my life and was wondering if I would speak with her brother, who was coming home on leave in a few weeks. I told her I would be glad to speak with him; obviously, I also noticed how good she looked!

When Mike came home, I went over to his house to pick him up. Cathy was going out on a date, but she made a point to come down and see me. I knew I was there that day to see her brother and to try to help him, but after looking at her, I knew I would be coming back, and not just to see her brother!

I spent a lot of time with Mike. He knew what I used to be like, and he saw the real change in my life. Mike was about to be discharged from the navy, and, as God would have it, Mike gave his life to Christ. God had made Himself real to him, and his whole world changed, just

> Jesus really does love everyone, and He wants to make Himself known to all people and become their Friend, their Lord, their Savior, and their King.

as mine had. It was beautiful to see how Jesus really does love everyone and how He wants to make Himself known to all people and become their Friend, their Lord, their Savior, and their King. Mike continues to serve the Lord to this day and is an outspoken instrument for the Lord everywhere he goes. I can remember the change in him like it was yesterday, and to see him today loving his family and serving God with his whole heart, it's just a beautiful thing to be a part of.

Well, as I was in the process of getting to know Mike, it happened that Cathy needed a ride to church one day, and I was all too happy to be at her service! I saw in her the virtues I was looking for in the woman I wanted to spend the rest of my life with. Cathy was not only beautiful on the outside, but she also had a passion for God that was genuine and a hunger for His Word that was awesome, and she loved to be around God's people.

Rick and his wife, Mary Jo, saw us together at church that day and asked us to come over for dinner (playing the matchmaker). Since I had simply offered to give Cathy a ride to church, they thought they would try to expand on that. We said yes, and from that point, we started dating. I fell madly in love with her right away, and I know this is going to sound really crazy, but I asked her to marry me two weeks after I first met her. I just couldn't imagine not spending the rest of my life with her. She had totally wrecked my world! I thought she was the most beautiful girl on earth, and there was no way I was going to take a chance that she would ever become someone else's wife.

To my surprise, she said yes, and then she asked me when I wanted to get married. I said soon, and she asked what "soon" meant to me. Since I had popped the question after just two weeks of dating, she didn't know what I was thinking. So, when I said two years, she looked at me like I was nuts. She was dumbfounded that I would first ask her to marry me after only two weeks of knowing her and then suggest that we get married after two years! When I saw her reaction, I asked what "soon" meant to her, and she rightfully said something like six months. We were married in less than six months, and that was thirty-five years ago. I don't recommend that others do that unless they are as sure as we were. All I can say is that Cathy is the best thing that ever happened in my life, after my coming to know Christ.

Today, we have three sons, three daughters-in-law, and three grandchildren. Cathy has been the tip of my compass to help me in my walk with God all these years. Her passion for God and her desire to serve Him have been the greatest examples to me of what it is to be a Christian. And her love for God, His Word, and His people has been an inspiration to many others. Having Cathy as my wife, with her constant, unyielding support for me and our family, has enabled me to be the man I am today.

10

A MAN'S GIFT MAKES ROOM FOR HIM

I had started school at Pitt, but I soon became disillusioned and decided to get a full-time job in sales. Although leaving school was a mistake I regret to this day, God really blessed my sales career, and things took off for me. The Bible says, *"A man's gift makes room for him, and brings him before great men"* (Proverbs 18:16). I had a natural desire to be around people, and the gifts that God had given me to deal with people were ideal for a sales and marketing career. So, things went very well for me, and I decided that this was the path that God had for my life.

This is not to say that everything was easy. Even though I had done well at the schools I had attended for my military training, starting in the business world with my sales jobs was a real struggle at first. Remember that, for most of the time during the last three years of my high school experience, my friends and I were either drinking or doing drugs, and the idea of education wasn't a priority. There were many instances when this lack of education created challenges for me later on.

Many of the things that other people took for granted were things I had difficulty with. At times, it was as though I was in a fog and just couldn't seem to break through. For example, at the beginning of my first sales job, I had trouble with even some simple calculations. Yet, through my having gone to school at Pitt, my participation in the discipleship group, and my personal Bible study time, God was slowly building me up in the areas I was lacking in, both in terms of education and from the effects of the alcohol. My time in God's Word was renewing and strengthening my mind.

God Will Provide for All Your Needs

I mention the above situation to you because I realize that not only will there be very successful people reading my story, people who had the opportunity for a great education and perhaps have never suffered with any addictions, but there also will be many other people who are struggling in certain ways today and just can't believe that their station in life could ever change. I can promise you this, because it comes from God's Word: "Ask and you will receive, seek and you will find; for everyone who will ask Me for help will receive, and everyone who seeks Me will find Me." (See Matthew 7:7–8.)

Matthew 6:6 says this:

But you, when you pray, go into your room, and when you have shut your door, pray to your Father who is in the secret place; and your Father who sees in secret will reward you openly.

You need to read the above verse again and again. God is your Creator and Father, and He wants you to talk with Him. The Creator of the universe wants you to shut your door and come and speak with Him in private and ask Him for the things you have need of. Even though He obviously knows what you need (see verse 32), He wants to speak with you about anything concerning you. How awesome is that? This truth captivates my mind with thoughts that cannot be described.

> Even though the Creator of the universe obviously knows what you need, He wants to speak with you about anything concerning you. How awesome is that?

God says we can ask Him for the things that we need, and He has promised to personally see to it that our needs are met. If you have a physical need, He can meet it. If you have an emotional need, He can meet it. If you have a financial need, He can meet it. If you have a loved one who is hurting or in some kind of trouble, He can meet that person's need.

God loves you and wants to walk with you. He will provide for whatever your need is because He loves you. How cool is that?

Speak and Act in the Name of Jesus

We'll talk more about the topic of faith and vocation in a later chapter, but I want to briefly talk about it here, too, in relation to where God led me in life after the Marines, because so many people feel that to have a full-time job rather than to be in full-time ministry is a "second place walk with God."

Well, it's not, and you must understand that if God has called you to be a businessperson, plumber, doctor, construction worker, car salesperson, lawyer, homemaker, or whatever your calling is, that means you are to do it with all your might as unto the Lord, from the heart, and not as unto man with just *"eye-service"* (Ephesians 6:6 NASB). *"And whatever you do in word or deed, do all in the name of the Lord Jesus, giving thanks to God the Father through Him"* (Colossians 3:17).

What you do every day means as much to God as what Billy Graham did in front of 100,000 people in a stadium somewhere!

What does that mean? Simply put, it means that by going to work every day and being faithful to God and trying to be the best witness for Him you can be, you will reach people who may never have gone to a church or an evangelistic meeting somewhere. God wants to flow through you wherever you are. He will bless the works of your hands and give you His favor with people wherever you go.

Any pastor or teacher of God's Word who has a biblically balanced perspective will teach this truth, and if you're hearing something different, it's not healthy for you. The church needs money to preach the gospel, and God always has His people in every walk of life. By having this attitude, I kept myself from having a Sunday-only mentality with my faith. I realized that God wanted to use me in the business world, and I was supposed to be the best I could be at my career. In doing so, I would honor Him.

Sure, others may make fun of you. The usual things will be said behind your back, such as "Oh, he's one of those born-againers," or "He's a Bible thumper." And yes, you will be put under a microscope, and, at times, everything you do will be looked at with a different set of rules. And when you do fail in your faith somehow, you'll hear, "I told you so; he's a phony." The thing I want you to understand is this: You're never going to be perfect, and when you do fail in your faith or just plain fail at anything, you need to be real with the people around you. They may have made jokes, but, at the end of the day, they know in their hearts that they have sin in their lives, and you are the one God is using to remind them of that, so this is one of the reasons they take the shots at you. Just love them and leave the results to God.

Remember, Jesus said that believers are like a city set on a hill; He said we are supposed to be light among the darkness. (See Matthew 5:14–16.) What happens when *you're* the person who flicks on the light switch in a dark room? People will always want to test your faith to see how much you really do believe in this God you claim to serve.

If you commit to being the best at what you do and ask God to bless the works of your hands, so that you can honor Him, you will always come out just fine. But remember, since you do claim to have this relationship with God, you need to honor Him with your work ethic and your integrity. Work harder, work smarter, try your hardest, and give it your best every day. Again, just be real with the people around you and love them where they are right now. Let go and let God do it for you. He will do a much better job than you ever could.

The book of Romans, which is in the New Testament, includes this verse: *"Not slothful in business; fervent in spirit; serving the Lord"* (Romans 12:11 KJV). I am sure one of the reasons the apostle Paul wrote this was that some of the Christians in Rome were being just that, "slothful." The word *"slothful"* in the Greek means "indolent." It carries the idea of a person who has a do-nothing, lethargic, lackadaisical, apathetic, indifferent, lukewarm attitude toward life.

I have hired Christians whom I knew had the potential to be really good and productive, but they had a lazy or idle attitude. I believe that a slothful outlook among Christians is one of the main reasons the world looks at the church as a pathetic entity made up of people who are just lazy losers. What an indictment against Christ and the things He stood for! Don't let that ever be said of you. Your attitude and work ethic are things you are totally in control of, and nobody or nothing can change them but you.

> If we are faithful in the little things, God will bless us in the greater things.

I have met many well-educated and well-trained people who would not be diligent in their daily habits and were always wondering why they could not seem to be successful like other people. The Bible tells us that if we are faithful in the little things, God will bless us in the greater things. (See Luke 19:17.) We have to prove our faithfulness in what we have been given to do right now, and then the thing that God has for us will come to light, and He will give us our hearts' desires.

Matthew 6:33 tells us, *"Seek first the kingdom of God and His righteousness, and all these things shall be added to you."*

What does that mean? It means that if we are truly trying to serve God the best we can and applying the principles taught in His Word, working diligently every day as unto the Lord from our hearts, we can rest in Him, knowing that all of our needs are going to be met.

An Unending Supply of God's Presence and Love

The second half of this book will go into greater detail about "What's Next?" now that you have become a Christian. These are things I have learned over the forty years I have been walking with God, and my prayer is that they will bless you and help you in your walk with Him, whether you have known Him for as long as I have or are a brand-new believer.

God has a journey prepared for you that is rich with His presence and His unending supply of love for you every step of the way. God asked Moses to do many things for Him, and the response Moses gave Him should be the cry of your heart. That response is, in effect, "God, I don't want to go anywhere Your presence does not go with me." (See Exodus 33:15.) God wants to walk with you every day in a very real and personal way; you just have to want Him to. Will you enter into His presence and His will for your life? Start right now by simply asking Jesus to come into your life, and He will pick you up and wrap you in His arms and cleanse you right where you are, right now!

Please say this simple prayer with me:

Father God, please forgive me for my sin and cleanse me through Jesus' death on the cross for me. Please, Jesus, come and live in my heart and help me to serve You. I need You, Jesus, and I want You to take control of my life and to be my Savior and my Lord. I surrender my soul to You. Let Your presence and love always go with me. In Jesus' name, amen.

Jim serving in the U.S. Marines, North Carolina, 1972

In the Mojave Desert for Marine training, 1972

Jim and Cathy,
wedding day,
June 1975

Raising their children
near Pittsburgh, PA

Jim and Cathy at a fund-raiser for the Nepal orphanage
where Cathy assists a missionary friend

Jim and Cathy with (*left to right*) grandchildren Lucy, James, and Dylan

The Maxim Family
Top row from left: son Jim, holding Dylan; son Jordan;
Jim, holding James; son John
Bottom row from left: daughter-in-law Alison; Cathy;
daughter-in-law Lauri, holding Lucy; daughter-in-law Jesica

PART TWO

JUST BETWEEN YOU AND ME

11

WHAT'S NEXT?

Around every bend in life, we ask the question, "What's next?" That is never truer than in the adventurous life of a Christian who wants to be used by God. If you want to make a difference in this life, the adventures your heavenly Father has for you will never stop. So, what's next?

I don't know where you are in your life right now. You may be worth millions, or you may be struggling to get by. You may live in a prison or a palace. But there's one thing I know: Jesus is standing at the door of your heart, waiting for you to open it. Do you remember the Scripture I found that first day in the bus station when I opened that little Bible?

> [Jesus said,] *Behold, I stand at the door and knock. If anyone hears My voice and opens the door, I will come in to him and dine with him, and he with Me.* (Revelation 3:20)

In part one of this book, you read about what Jesus did for me. He came to me and knocked on the door of my heart when I didn't want to hear from Him or from anyone else about what God desired for me. You read how He came to me in the darkest hour of my life and forgave me. But maybe you think you've gone too far and Jesus could not or would not want to love you and forgive you for what you've done or who you've become. Or, maybe you are so well off financially that you just don't feel a need for God. Maybe you're thinking all this stuff about Christianity and the need for a Savior is for people who are beneath you in some way. Well, just give me a few more minutes of your time and read the story of a man who was a king and had both financial security *and* darkness in his life.

A FALLEN WARRIOR

The Bible gives us the account of one of the most prominent men in recorded history. His name was David, and his story is found in the Old Testament, in the book of 2 Samuel, chapter 11. According to the Bible, from his earliest years, David was a man after God's own heart. (See Acts 13:22.) Learning that, you may think he was a really holy guy who never made a mistake. Well, read on.

David was Israel's king, and his army was out fighting a war with the sons of Ammon to defend Israel. (Some things haven't changed over the centuries!) It was the custom for the king to go out with the army to ensure the victory, but, this time, David decided to stay home, even though he knew he belonged with his fighting men. While David was standing on his rooftop deck looking out over the capital city of Jerusalem, he noticed a very beautiful woman bathing on a nearby rooftop. When he asked his servants who she was, he discovered she was Bathsheba, the wife of Uriah, one of his most faithful warriors.

Obviously, a man after God's own heart should have moved his eyes and his heart away from that tempting scene. Instead, David commanded that she be brought to him. The servants brought Bathsheba, she had sex with the king, and she became pregnant. Now, you might be thinking that David would confess his actions and do something to take care of her, right? Wrong.

King David tried to fix the situation with cover-ups and deception, just like many of us today are guilty of. He sent for Uriah from the battlefield and told him that he had earned a break from the fighting and a night to spend with his wife. David intended to cover his tracks. If Uriah spent the night with Bathsheba, then he would think that the baby was his, and no one would know of David's sin.

Uriah went home, but instead of going to spend the night with his wife, he slept outside. He was too honorable to indulge in marital pleasure while his buddies were still in danger. Uriah was a real man's man and very loyal to his king. Now, in my mind, Uriah is the guy who was a man after God's own heart!

When David heard of Uriah's decision, he tried another tactic. He got Uriah drunk to weaken his resolve so he would go in to sleep with his wife. It still didn't work! Uriah chose to sleep outside David's castle with the king's servants.

At that point, David made the worst decision of his life. He wrote a letter to Joab, his army commander, and gave it to Uriah to carry back to the battlefield. The letter ordered Joab to place Uriah on the front line of the fiercest battle and then to pull the army back. Uriah would be standing alone and would die in battle. This was far worse than "friendly fire"; this was the planned murder of one of his own men! David would complete his deception with this one treacherous act.

Joab was a faithful commander, and he obeyed David's orders without question. Uriah was killed in battle, and Joab sent word back to the king that the deed had been accomplished. But which one was the fallen warrior, Uriah or David? In my opinion, it was David.

> David forgot how God loved him too much to let him get away with sin. Not dealing with sin in our lives will eventually ruin us.

Now David thought it was all cleaned up, right? He thought nobody would ever find out about his immoral actions with Bathsheba. But David forgot about the God he served and how God loved him too much to let him get away with sin. God knows that not dealing with sin in our lives will eventually ruin us.

Quite truthfully, no matter how we try to deny it, there is nothing hidden away from the sight of our Creator. In David's case, God sent a prophet named Nathan to convict David of the gravity of what he had done. Nathan related a sad story of a rich man who had many sheep and one poor guy who had only one lamb. The rich man had a visitor for dinner, and instead of feeding his guest with one of his many sheep, he took the poor man's one and only lamb and killed it for the meal.

Nathan looked at David and asked, in effect, "What do you think about this?" David became enraged and wanted to have the greedy man executed for his actions. Nathan looked David in the eye and said words like this: "David, *you* are that man! You had Uriah killed so that you could take his wife. Because of your sin, the baby she gave birth to will die." David was convicted of the full weight of his sin! (See 2 Samuel 12:1–14.)

It's Called Grace, and It's Amazing!

I know the question is, "How was this guy a man after God's own heart?"

In my book, David should have been shot for what he did. It doesn't make sense to me that God would call him a man after His own heart. Well, the good news is that the Bible tells us our ways are not the same as the Lord's ways. *"As the heavens are higher than the earth, so are My ways higher than your ways"* (Isaiah 55:9). God looks into a man's heart and then grants him the grace to repent of his sins.

David recognized his sin for what it was; he repented of, or turned from, that sin and then asked for forgiveness from God—and God forgave him. David wrote his prayer for forgiveness in Psalm 51. Here is a portion of that prayer:

> *Have mercy upon me, O God....Wash me thoroughly from my iniquity, and cleanse me from my sin. For I acknowledge my transgressions, and my sin is always before*

me. Against You, You only, have I sinned, and done this evil in Your sight....Hide Your face from my sins, and blot out all my iniquities. Create in me a clean heart, O God, and renew a steadfast spirit within me.

(Psalm 51:1–4, 9–10)

Please read this entire psalm so that you will see David's heartfelt desire to receive cleansing and forgiveness.

I know this kind of forgiveness can be hard to believe, and sometimes it sounds too easy and too cheap. David should have paid a heavy price for what he did to Uriah, and because of his sin, his baby died. But God, in His mercy and forgiveness, gives us sinners another chance. That chance became possible through the death of Jesus Christ as the sacrifice for our sins. *He* paid the heavy price so that *we* could be forgiven. It's called grace, and *it is amazing!*

> God promises that we are not beyond His forgiveness. We are saved by the grace that He freely gives us; we are not saved by how much we work to be better.

Good News!

The Bible says that we are all sinners, falling short of the holiness of God. (See Romans 3:23.) Yet He promises that we are not beyond His hand of forgiveness. We are saved by the grace that God freely gives us; we are not saved by how much we work to be better. *"For by grace you have been saved through faith, and that not of yourselves; it is the gift of God, not of works, lest anyone should boast"* (Ephesians 2:8–9).

God gave His only Son, Jesus Christ, so that whoever calls on His name can receive forgiveness for ALL of his sins.

In the New Testament, Paul gave us the great news of our salvation: *"If you confess with your mouth the Lord Jesus and believe in your heart that God has raised Him from the dead, you will be saved.... For 'whoever calls on the name of the LORD shall be saved'"* (Romans 10:9, 13).

Whether you are the person in prison right now who feels that you are beyond God's love, or you are the rich man who thinks you don't need to be saved, remember, David experienced both of those situations. Yet, God forgave him and gave him and Bathsheba another son, whom they named Solomon. Solomon became the king of Israel and the wisest and richest man who ever lived.

I remember a gentleman with whom I was doing some business who was the president of a rather large association of some prominent professionals. I had a product at that time that was fairly popular, and we put together a joint marketing effort for all the members of his association. The members of his group would not only use the product themselves but also market it to their customers.

This gentleman was a very polished individual who had a great education and came from a fairly wealthy family. He was always a private person; in fact, he had a completely "buttoned-up" personality. We had developed a friendship over a few years, and, once in a while, we would have lunch or play golf together. I had tried sharing my faith with him several times, but all I'd ever received from him in response were a few nods and silence. One day, we had lunch together. By this time, I had known the Lord for many years, and if I'd ever learned anything about sharing my faith, it was that I must wait upon the Holy Spirit to open the doors, and then He would lead me through them.

We had just finished lunch, and I was driving him back to his office, when something started happening within me. I had been a Christian for many years, and I knew it was the leading of God's Spirit. I pulled into the parking space, but even though we had finished our business meeting, I could tell there was something on his mind. Remember, I had shared my faith with him many times in a low-key manner, waiting for him to respond, but he would never go near "that conversation."

Another friend of mine who had played golf with us told me after he met this guy that he was one of the most uptight people he had ever met, and in fact he was. My friend said that this guy was like a piece of granite and wanted no one in his "space"—and he let you know it.

But I knew today was different because, typically, when God's Spirit is leading me, I begin to feel a great compassion for the person I am speaking with, and my only desire is for that person to experience the love God has for him or her. I don't have any "agenda" other than for the person to receive God's love.

As we were sitting in the parking space, I looked over at him and said, "Tom, God loves you," and, with that, he started weeping, right there in my front seat. I mean, weeping uncontrollably. The presence of God was so real that it was as if both of us had a blanket of love resting on us. God began pouring out His love all over Tom, and Tom was asking God to cleanse him and forgive him.

This went on for about twenty minutes or so, and then I shared with him some Scriptures to show him in writing just how much God loved him. I find it very meaningful to people to show them God's Word and not just tell them how much God loves them because, after all, it's God's love and His power, not mine, that has brought them to salvation, and Tom, too, received Christ that day.

I spent time with Tom, reading the Bible and praying with him, and he began to sense God calling him to the ministry full-time! He wanted to quit his job and go to Bible school or seminary and spend the rest of his life telling others about his faith and how much God loves people. When I described Tom's conversion to my friend who had compared him to a piece of granite, we both marveled at the grace of God.

I introduced Tom to some pastors I knew, recognizing that they could help him with some of the decisions he was wrestling with. Tom did end up going to Bible school, and today he is leading a ministry sharing God's love with people everywhere he goes. How cool is that!

I have never experienced anything in the world that can remotely compare to sharing God's love with someone and watching that

> I have never experienced anything that can remotely compare to sharing God's love with someone and watching that person be transformed before my very eyes.

person be transformed before my very eyes. I never get tired of seeing God draw people to Himself, and if that means I have to get ridiculed or be made fun of or be considered just another one of those "born-againers," then so be it. I can't help sharing God's love with people, because He first loved me and forgave me of all my sins.

As I wrote earlier, I've made mistakes while sharing my faith, especially in my early years of walking with God. Sometimes, I had no business opening my mouth about Jesus without being led to by the Holy Spirit, and sometimes I was "pushing my own agenda," and for that, I'm truly sorry. Like anything else, you learn from your mistakes and ask for forgiveness and move on. Over the years that I have walked with God, I have had many encounters with people just like Tom, with whom God gave me appointments in order to share His love. It's the greatest joy I have ever known and something that I long to experience even now.

I have said this before in the course of this book, but if you are sensing God pulling on the strings of your heart, please stop right now and ask Him to cleanse you and forgive you through Jesus' sacrifice on the cross for you. Ask Jesus Christ to come into your life, and He will love you, wrap His arms around you, and fill you with His love. Please don't let anything stop you from surrendering your heart to God. He wants only one thing from you, and that's your heart. He loves you so much that He sent His only Son to die for your sins and for mine. Just say, "Father, forgive me for all that I've done and cleanse me of my sin. Jesus, come and live within my heart."

If you are a believer, and your walk with Christ has grown a little stale or cold, or maybe your spiritual life is in a rut, God wants to minister to you right now. He can restore you and give you back the spark you once had to share His love with people around you. God wants to renew your "secret place" of prayer and usher you back into His presence. Just ask Him to forgive you for anything that is between you and Him and let Him pour out His Holy Spirit on you to refresh and revitalize you. He longs to have that closeness with you again.

There's an old hymn written by a man who knew just how much God had forgiven him, and these are some of the words:

> There is a fountain filled with blood
> Drawn from Immanuel's veins;
> And sinners plunged beneath that flood
> Lose all their guilty stains.[1]

The Bible says, *"There is no other name under heaven given among men by which we must be saved"* (Acts 4:12), and that name is Jesus Christ.

So, here's the whole point: It's not what we do to make God love us and forgive us; it's the sacrifice Jesus paid on the cross and the blood He shed for all of us that God sees when we turn our lives over to Him. Whenever we call on Jesus and ask Him to forgive us and cleanse us, He will come running to our sides and forgive us. Then, He will come into our hearts and live with us forever. When we die, we can be sure that we will spend eternity with Him. God's grace and forgiveness have to sound like good news to you! I know they were great news to me, and I'm sure they were great news to David.

---

[1] William Cowper, "There Is a Fountain Filled with Blood," 1772.

If you are someone who is very comfortable with the financial position you are in, or with your business or your status in the community, remember that, as the king, David had it all, too. Don't wait until some calamity jolts you awake before you realize how frail you really are. One small blood clot breaking loose in your system could end your life in a second. You know deep down that God loves you and has been knocking on the door of your heart. Today can be the time for you to open that door and ask Jesus to cleanse you and forgive you. Now can be the start of a brand-new day in your life. Let God love you and be the heavenly Father He longs to be to you.

> Let God love you and be the heavenly Father He longs to be to you.

Jesus died on the cross for your sins and mine. If you would only humble yourself and ask Him to come into your life, He will make everything new. That's what being born again is all about—Jesus taking the throne of your life and cleansing and forgiving you...forever.

12

No Limit to Jesus' Reach

I boarded an early morning flight, as I had done hundreds of times before, only this time, I would witness one of the greatest miracles I have ever seen. The plane was a 727 jet, and, as I walked through the doorway, the flight attendant said good morning, as they always do. I glanced at the cockpit as usual and then headed to my seat.

Normally, I try to sit in a row next to an emergency exit, for the additional leg room. As I looked down the long aisle, I saw only one other passenger on the entire plane! It was another man, and he was sitting in the very last row. I was dumbfounded...a completely empty jet! Puzzled, I took my seat and was reminded of my customary morning prayer time. That very morning, before I had gotten on the plane, I had prayed a simple prayer like this: *Father God, in the name of Jesus, please use me today to make faith come alive in someone's heart, somewhere. Lord, please help me share Your love with somebody today.*

Immediately, I thought that God had emptied an entire flight so that the man in the back of the plane could hear about God's love for him. I was so excited that I could hardly wait to get back to him, introduce myself, and start some small talk with him. I looked forward to seeing how the Holy Spirit would lead this encounter and what the outcome would be. I had been walking with the Lord for many years by this point, and He had put me in some incredible situations just to reach people with His love and salvation. I just knew that this was one of those times, and I was jumping out of my skin with excitement.

Lord, give me wisdom to talk with him, I prayed. I started thinking about people who'd had others praying for them, and then God, in answer to their prayers, had rearranged everything in those people's lives just so they could hear the gospel. How much God must love this man on the plane that He would arrange an encounter like this!

He must be the most prayed-for man I have ever met! I thought. *Who was his mother? Or was it his wife, sister, or brother who was praying? Who could it be that was on their knees for his soul? To empty an entire flight! What a statement of God's faithfulness and unending love to reach a soul this way!* I was restless for the plane to take off so I could get to the back and watch this miracle unfold before me.

The plane reached cruising altitude, and I started to take off my seatbelt. At that point, the flight attendant walked up and very politely asked me if there was anything she could get for me. I said, "No, thanks." She then asked if I would like some breakfast, and I said, "No, thank you," once again. Not to be put off, she asked me a third time if I wanted any coffee or orange juice.

I started to get a little annoyed. After all, I had a God-ordained appointment with the man in the back, and she was distracting me. Suddenly, it was as if the Holy Spirit hit me on the back of the head and said, *It's not him, dummy; it's her!*

> Suddenly, it was as if the Holy Spirit hit me on the back of the head and said, *It's not him, dummy; it's her!*

I'm sure my eyes widened about two inches and my mouth dropped open! It was unbelievable what was happening here. With a completely different expression, I responded to her, "I think I'll have some coffee, and while you're at it, I'll take some orange juice, as well!" As she turned to walk away, I felt God's overwhelming presence and quickly started praying. Sometimes, sharing the gospel with women when I am by myself can be tricky, with the dynamics of talking to a woman you have never met before and all that. But, when I am sure God has ordained the moment, I get all green lights and move forward in faith.

As she handed me the drinks, we started laughing about the plane being empty and how she had her own jet. While we talked, I knew in my spirit that this young woman had been marked by God to hear His message of love and forgiveness today, right now, on this plane, at 30,000 feet!

Even though I'd had several encounters like this in my life—"God moments"—seldom had I ever felt more strongly the presence of God to share His love with someone. As always, my mind went back to the moment in my life when I lay in a pool of my own blood, facing the powers of darkness, with my life in the balance. The moment when God stepped in and rescued me when I least deserved it. The moment when all hell had taken me captive and there was no way out but Jesus. Was she facing that moment right now?

She asked me how I had started my business; I answered her briefly, and then I said, "I'm very thankful for the way things have turned out and how God has blessed me with a beautiful wife and three sons." I saw the look come over her, as I had seen it come over others so many times before. The look tells me they are reflecting on something very deep in their own hearts. So I spoke again, "I bet you have a lot of things to be thankful for," and right then she just stopped. It was like she was frozen in time. Her eyes closed, and the tears started flowing down her cheeks like Niagara Falls. Soon, her makeup was running down her face as she tried to look at me.

"You have a mother at home praying for you, don't you?" I asked quietly. "It's time to come home today. God has emptied the entire plane and rearranged US Air's schedule just for you." Both of us were in total awe of the power of God's love. We felt His presence; we knew He was standing right there with us.

I continued, "You've been running long enough; it's time to surrender to His love for you." She just kept on weeping, and I was watching the greatest miracle in the kingdom of heaven. I knew the angels were rejoicing, and I knew her mom's prayers were being answered right before my eyes.

It was one of the holiest moments of my life. Neither of us could move. God Himself had reached down from heaven and wrapped His arms around her and was showering His love and peace and forgiveness all over her, and I was so privileged to have a front-row seat for it all. I was encouraged once again by God's love for me and all of His children. I sat there in complete reverence, reflecting on His unending love. Nobody, *absolutely nobody*, is beyond His reach.

> God Himself reached down from heaven and showered His love, peace, and forgiveness over her. Nobody, *absolutely nobody*, is beyond His reach.

I prayed with her, and she rededicated her life to Jesus. I then encouraged her to call her mom right away. She promised to get back into Christian fellowship and Bible study, surrounding herself with other believers who could encourage her in her walk with Christ.

It was hard to have this time in God's presence come to an end. But, now, the encounter was over, and her new walk in Christ was just beginning. I told her that if God could empty a plane to get to her, He was more than capable of directing her everyday life! She shouldn't worry about anything!

I walked off that plane in complete amazement. The airport terminal actually became a sanctuary for me as I sat alone for a while, reflecting on what had just occurred. I didn't want to speak with anyone or go anywhere but just drink in the mercy and love of God—the almighty God who had emptied an entire aircraft in response to a mother's prayers.

This can be the moment for your encounter with the same all-powerful, loving, kind, compassionate God. It's no coincidence that you are reading this chapter right now. God has rearranged your schedule for you to read this book, the same way He rearranged the airline's schedule to bring that young woman back to Himself.

> Today is your God-appointed moment to come home to Him. God is knocking on the door of your heart right now; will you let Him in?

Today, right now, is your God-appointed moment to come home to Him. God is knocking on the door of your heart right now; will you please let Him in? Will you bow your heart to Him right now and ask Him to forgive you and cleanse you from your sin and bring you back to Himself? He longs to walk close to you and love you and be your best Friend. Jesus died on a cross and suffered for you and for me so that we could be in close fellowship with Him.

If you have prayed that prayer, you can rest assured that God will rearrange the rest of your life to take care of you. I know that someone is praying for you, so go and tell that person who comes to your mind today that you have asked Christ into your life to forgive and cleanse you. Just let God shine in your life, and the rest will all fall into place. Remember, He has your address.

13

YOU ARE NOT ALONE!

How can you grow stronger? How can you remain free from the life God has just rescued you from? How can you begin to grow as a new Christian and start telling others that Jesus forgave you and cleansed you? How can you learn the Bible and become an effective "soldier of the cross," spiritually speaking? (See 2 Timothy 2:3–4.)

Well, first, there is more good news—*you are not alone*! God never intended for us to have to do any of this by ourselves. In fact, we *cannot* do it by ourselves; it takes the supernatural power of God to enable us to serve Him on a daily basis. He has initiated His love for you by drawing you to Himself. Jesus said, *"You did not choose Me, but I chose you and appointed you that you should go and bear fruit, and that your fruit should remain, that whatever you ask the Father in My name He may give you"* (John 15:16).

Since God, your Father, has been knocking on the door of your heart, if you have responded to His call on your life, He is not about to say to you, "Now, it's up to you; go figure it all out!" God has given us His plan for our lives, and we find it in His Word.

Remember when I described first picking up the Bible at the bus station on my way to Parris Island, and how it was as if I was drinking from a fire hose? Now, it's your turn to let God teach you about Himself. Spend time with the *almighty God*— the God who created the universe! Yes, that's what I said: the God who created the universe! He longs to spend time with you. You can have a daily appointment with the most awesome, most powerful, most creative, most compassionate, most wise, and most loving God—who also happens to be your heavenly Father. He wants you to have the privilege of coming to Him every day. And, what's more, He provides a radical Helper and Teacher to guide you in this relationship with Him!

Who Is This Radical Helper and Teacher?

Near the end of His life on earth, Jesus let His disciples know that it was time for Him to leave them and rejoin His Father in heaven, but He also gave them a vital promise:

> But now I go away to Him who sent Me, and none of you asks Me, "Where are you going?" But because I have said these things to you, sorrow has filled your heart. Nevertheless I tell you the truth. **It is to your advantage** that I go away; for if I do not go away, the Helper will not come to you; but if I depart, **I will send Him to you**.
>
> (John 16:5–7, emphasis added)

When I speak to you about God coming into your heart, it is because Jesus promised to send Someone who would live within us as a Helper and Teacher, as well as a Comforter and Deliverer. That *Someone* is the Holy Spirit. The word *"Helper"* in the passage from John 16 actually means "one who comes alongside to help."

The Bible says, in effect, "Don't you realize that now that you have given your life to God, your body is a living temple of the Holy Spirit?" (See 1 Corinthians 6:19.) God lives within you by His Holy Spirit.

Who exactly is this Helper—this Holy Spirit? He is the third Person of the Godhead—a member of the Trinity of God the Father, God the Son (Jesus), and God the Holy Spirit. In that Trinity, the Holy Spirit is equal to God the Father and to Jesus. His role is to live with us on earth as a Helper, just as Jesus and the Father have Their roles in heaven. Some of the Holy Spirit's actions on this earth are listed below:

- The Holy Spirit "seals" us into the body of Christ (see Ephesians 1:13–14), making us a precious and important part of God's church. *"For by one Spirit we were all baptized into one body....Now you are the body of Christ, and members individually"* (1 Corinthians 12:13, 27).

- The Holy Spirit *"makes intercession"* for us when we don't know how to pray. When we don't know how to voice our deepest needs to God, the Holy Spirit can cry out to Him for us. *"For we do not know what we should pray for as we*

ought, but the Spirit Himself makes intercession for us with groanings which cannot be uttered....He makes intercession
for the saints according to the will of God"
(Romans 8:26–27).

- The Holy Spirit empowers us to go into
  the world as effective witnesses for Jesus
  Christ. *"But you shall receive power when
  the Holy Spirit has come upon you; and
  you shall be witnesses to Me in Jerusalem, and in all Judea and Samaria, and to
  the end of the earth"* (Acts 1:8).

- The Holy Spirit searches the things of
  God and reveals them to us as His children. First Corinthians 2:9–12 tells us
  that the Spirit searches the truths of
  the Father and then teaches them to us,
  *"that we might know the things that have
  been freely given to us by God"* (verse 12).

- The Holy Spirit speaks to us in a still,
  small voice. (See 1 Kings 19:12.) How does
  this happen? The Holy Spirit will guide
  us by speaking softly to our hearts. This
  isn't something strange; it is simply knowing in your heart that your thoughts are
  inspired by Him. The Holy Spirit's guidance will never go against the teachings
  of the Bible. The more time you spend in
  the Word, the more you will recognize the
  Holy Spirit's guidance.

Now that you have given your life to Christ, it
is vital that you truly understand the following: God
gave us His Holy Spirit to live within us, to guide us,

to walk with us daily, and to communicate God's love to us. God never intended for us to walk through this life alone!

Let the Holy Spirit Guide You Daily

Jesus told us the Holy Spirit was sent to do even more:

> I still have many things to say to you, but you cannot bear them now. However, when He, the Spirit of truth, has come, **He will guide you into all truth**; for He will not speak on His own authority, but **whatever He hears He will speak**; and He will tell you things to come. **He will glorify Me, for He will take of what is Mine and declare it to you**. All things that the Father has are Mine. Therefore I said that He will take of Mine and declare it to you.
> (John 16:12–15, emphasis added)

These were some of Jesus' last words while He was here on earth. If you were in Jesus' position, and you were leaving the earth physically, with a new era about to begin, wouldn't you talk to your disciples about the things that were most important?

Letting His disciples know that Someone was coming to help them was the most important message on Jesus' heart. He assured them, *"I will not leave you orphans; I will come to you"* (John 14:18). He said these words to comfort them and to encourage them—they would have the ability to live in victory!

When you gave your life to Jesus, the Holy Spirit came into your heart, and, at that moment, you were born again. Now that you are a Christian, you want the Holy Spirit to teach you the things of God. Again, the Holy Spirit will be your Guide, your Comforter, and your Teacher every day.

RESPONDING TO THE HOLY SPIRIT'S LEADING

Sometimes, I sense the Holy Spirit prompting me to speak with someone, either to share my faith or to give a word of encouragement. What do I mean when I say, "I sense the Holy Spirit prompting me to speak with someone"? If you don't know Christ yet, or if you are a new believer, you may wonder what I am referring to. Well, above, I wrote that the Holy Spirit was given to us by God to be our Guide, our Comforter, and our Teacher, and that He speaks to us in a "still, small voice." I mentioned that if we will spend time with God in prayer and in studying His Word, then our spirits, our brains, our emotions, and our hearts will become more "in tune" with God, and we can develop a sensitivity to the presence of His Holy Spirit in our lives and to what He is conveying to us. We can learn to listen for His leading about what He wants us to do at a certain time.

> If you spend time with God in prayer and studying His Word, you can develop a sensitivity to the presence of the Holy Spirit in your life and what He is conveying to you.

I seldom have heard an audible voice from God in the forty years that I have been walking with Him.

I don't need to hear a voice from God because He has given us His Word to study and meditate upon. As I said earlier, all of the Holy Spirit's guidance will always line up perfectly with God's Word—He would never ask us to do something contrary to the truths and principles of the Bible. Get to know God's Word thoroughly; meditate upon it day and night. (See Joshua 1:8.) Become a student, a lifelong learner, of His Word. It is our guide and barometer for every decision.

I think that when we Christians say something to our friends like "God told me," or "I heard God say such and such," we can do harm to our witness to them because it sounds as if we hear Him audibly all the time. Now, God can do anything He wants to, anytime He wants to, because He is God. So, He might speak to us audibly at times. However, most of the time, when I feel God is leading me to do something, it is a deep impression upon my heart and mind. And I have learned that I need to rely on God's strength and power for whatever is about to happen, rather than trying to do it myself without continuing to listen to Him and waiting for His leading. It is very important for me to know that I am not doing this in my own power and that it's not somehow "my great talents and abilities" that can accomplish this task. Yielding myself to God and asking Him to make me sensitive to Him for what He might want me to say or do is the most important thing.

Maybe you're thinking, *Look, Maxim, God gave me a brain, so if it's to be, it's up to me! I don't need to ask God every waking moment of every day for His leading and get all spooky and spiritual and stuff!*

Or, perhaps you're thinking, *Maxim, there are three kinds of people in the world: those who make things happen, those who watch things happen, and those who don't know what's happening. And I'm going to be the first kind of person!*

If you're thinking something like the above, bear with me for a moment. I am not saying that I go about my everyday life paralyzed to accomplish things if I "don't feel His leading." What I am saying is this: I want to be used by God to help and bless other people in any way that I can, and He knows how I should go about doing that.

In the past, I have often stepped out in my own desire to help someone or to rush into a situation because it seemed like the natural thing to do, since I tend to be a man of action. But I know the human tendency to develop an ego that says, "It's all about me." It's easy to think, *I don't need God to do anything. I know what to do here. I can figure it out. I can get this thing done.* Or, we may say to someone—or just think it—"Move over; I'll take care of that."

> God has equipped us with certain talents. Yet, if you want to be used by God long-term, you must be willing to acknowledge it is God who is working in you.

In contrast, waiting upon God for His leading honors Him because it indicates, "Father, I want to do Your will. I want to be used by You to bless people *in order to bring You the honor and glory due Your name.*"

It's true that God has equipped us with certain talents and gifts. Yet, if you want to be used by God long-term, you must be willing to have a heart attitude that acknowledges it is God who is working in you, and not you doing things according to your own talents and strengths.

Many a preacher, teacher, or pastor who has fallen into sin (and we have all seen or heard about them) fell because he became the center of attraction rather than giving the prominence to God. God will not share His glory with anyone. (See, for example, Isaiah 42:8.) He alone is God, and He alone is worthy. Honoring Him by asking Him to make you sensitive to His Holy Spirit will keep your heart teachable to His ways.

Timely Words

Let me tell you about an instance when the Holy Spirit prompted me to minister to someone, and I had to rely on Him totally. I was the one of the Royal Ranger "Commanders" in my church. Royal Rangers is like the Boy Scouts, only with a spiritual emphasis, in addition to all the outdoor activities and the normal things you teach boys. We were on weekend camping trip, and the boys were doing an activity, and it was my time to take a short break. I felt like taking a walk through the woods to get a little breather from having twenty kids hanging on me all the time!

After I'd walked around for a while, I noticed a young guy who looked to be in his early twenties under a pavilion, and he seemed to be praying. I didn't recognize him as one of the Royal Ranger leaders, and since he was praying, I was just going to leave him alone and keep walking. But then, I felt the Holy Spirit prompting me to go and speak with this man.

I didn't know what God would have me say to him; I just knew I was supposed to talk with him.

It was obvious that this was one of those "divine appointments," and now things began to get serious in my spirit. What would happen shortly would change the future for many people. As I approached him, I saw that he was really seeking God about some things. He seemed to hear me coming, but he kept praying. I walked closer to him and just put my hand on his shoulder. Immediately, I felt the presence of God in a very strong way, and I started praying. He must have felt the presence of God, too, because he began to weep. He then began to sob. His heart was so heavy that I knew the only thing for me to do was to shut up and pray silently. At this point, I really sensed that I was in over my head, and I knew that God had to show up in a big way and tell me what to do, because this young man needed something that was far beyond the natural. I didn't know who he was or what God had in store for him, but I knew enough about God's methods by now to know that this young man had a destiny to be fulfilled and that God had designed it so that I was going to be a part of it in some small way.

As we were praying, it was if God, through His Holy Spirit, enfolded us in His power and strength, so that we were speechless and in total awe that He was visiting us in this manner. This young man's name was Tom, and I asked him to tell you in his own words what happened that day:

"Before I'd left for the camp, I had prayed, *Lord, why in the world did I commit to speaking to a bunch of middle-class Christian Boy Scouts in the middle of the woods, when my heart is to stay right here today and reach the 'forgotten' kids that I love so much in West Philadelphia?*

"My thoughts to God reflected my frustrations of trying so hard to help children in the inner city know the love of Jesus and break out of the cycle of poverty, addictions, and crime, with little noticeable change. As a newlywed couple, my wife, Lois, and I had given so much effort to making a difference, and yet we felt as though we had not seen the transformation in the community that we had passionately desired. I had been feeling like a complete failure.

"Now, I felt like I was abandoning these underprivileged children, who never had the chance to enjoy a three-day camping experience, for a 'getaway' with total strangers who just wanted to be entertained with a few adventurous stories from a young 'ghetto' preacher. I knew my attitude needed a divine adjustment. What I didn't know was that God had arranged a divine appointment that would change my life forever.

"When I arrived at the campground, the leader of the event kindly greeted me and showed me the tent where I would be sleeping. He provided me with a sleeping bag and all the gear I needed for the weekend. What he didn't provide was a wet suit, which I soon wished I'd brought with me!

"With the Royal Ranger powwow lasting just a couple of days,

"God wasted no time prepping me for the divine appointment. First things first: the attitude adjustment came quickly."

God wasted no time prepping me for the divine appointment. First things first: the attitude adjustment came quickly. The first night of the weekend, it rained cats and dogs. It was just what I needed to soften my city-hardened heart. I happened to be 'lucky' enough to get the corner of the tent where all the water settled. Instead of a sleeping bag, I should have had a canoe. I was soaked to the bone. Not wanting to draw attention to myself, I quietly left the tent for my car. I changed my clothes and did my best to stay warm for the rest of the night.

"'Lord, You've got my attention. What am I doing here?' I asked. The Lord whispered to my heart, *Do you believe that I order your steps?* 'Yes, Lord!' I replied. *Good. Trust Me. I have a reason for your being here. Tomorrow, you'll know what it is.*

"After breakfast the next morning, I felt led by the Holy Spirit to find a quiet spot to pray, away from the morning's activities and competitions of the boys' camp. I took a walk in the woods, settled in under the shelter of a wooden pavilion, and began to call on God. I asked God to speak to me. Although I was just twenty-five years old, I knew I was at a crossroads and in desperate need of God's help.

"I don't remember how long I had been praying when, suddenly, I heard a few footsteps and realized that someone had just joined me. Within moments, there was an incredible sense of God's holy presence. I wept as the Holy Spirit began to expose the sins in my life, such as pride, bitterness, unforgiveness, and selfish ambition. I felt so unworthy, so ashamed.

"It was at this time that a man I had never met began to tell me exactly what I was thinking and the hurts that I had experienced. He began to share with me in detail how much God loved me and how He had a great destiny for my life.

"As I heard the words about God's love for me, I began to sob uncontrollably. I believe this meeting with Jim Maxim in the presence of almighty God was the reason why I was in the woods of Pennsylvania for a three-day weekend. God introduced me to His messenger, who would become my friend for life. Amazingly, God has continued to use Jim to speak into my life at every significant crossroads of our ministry. Yes, the meeting of two men in the woods was definitely an appointment designed by God.

"This divine appointment had an immediate and lasting effect on my life. When I returned home, my precious wife met me at the door of our one-room apartment. As soon as she saw me, she asked with wonder, 'What happened this weekend?' I said, 'What do you mean?' and she said, 'You look so different, so peaceful, so relaxed.'

"God used Jim Maxim to speak His timely word to a young man who was frustrated by broken promises and broken dreams. Jim brought God's love to a young 'ghetto' preacher with a broken heart, and God's love produced His peace, a peace that passes all understanding.

"Since that time, Lois and I have had the privilege to serve in missions for over twenty-five years around the world. From inner-city Philadelphia to Prague, Czech Republic, our experience has included street evangelism, Teen Challenge, Turning Point, church planting, radio evangelism, and children's ministries. In God's providence, we have been able to partner with our friends Jim and Cathy Maxim for several special ministry opportunities. Our current assignment is leading Convoy of Hope's global prayer initiative for the poor and suffering.

"James 1:17 says, *'Every good and perfect gift is from above'* (NIV). The gift of God's peace given to me in the woods many years ago still guards my heart and mind through Christ Jesus. And the gift of Jim's friendship continues to grace the ministry God has called me to. All of it beginning with a divine appointment of two men meeting in the woods of Pennsylvania. To God be all the glory!"

GOD WANTS ALL OF YOU!

God wants to have all of you. The more you yield to Him, the more you become like Him. When people around you see God in your life, they will want to know how they can meet the God who saved and changed you. The question is not how we can get more of God, but rather, how we can give more of ourselves to Him. Yield yourself to Him daily, hourly, moment by moment, and ask Him to live big in you. Ask Him never to let you limit Him in your life. Ask Him to use you everywhere you go to bring people to the cross and to make faith come alive in them. Ask Him to make you sensitive to His Holy Spirit within you and to cleanse you and forgive you when you fall. Run to Him when you stumble, rather than running away, as you have before.

> The question is not how we can get more of God, but rather, how we can give more of ourselves to Him.

Here is another account of how the Holy Spirit directed me to share God's love with someone. One time, I was driving home from work and saw a man hitchhiking. Now, I do not encourage too many people to pick up strangers, and I don't do it as often as I used to, but, in this instance, I felt like I was supposed to give this man a ride.

He jumped in the car, and I asked him where he was headed. It was right on my way home. I noticed he had many tattoos on his arms, and he was obviously a weight lifter and just rough-looking. We starting making small talk, and he said his car was getting repaired. I replied, "Well, thank God for your health, anyway," just to bring God into the conversation as fast as I could and see what reaction I would get. He seemed to pause when I said this and mumbled something like, "I don't know much about God."

Well, to someone who had prayed that morning and asked God to use him to make faith come alive in someone's heart that day, the door was wide open. I began to tell him the story of Jesus! I told him how Jesus came to earth to die for us so we could be forgiven. I told him how much God loved him and wanted to walk with him and be his Friend. I told him it didn't matter what he had done in his life because Jesus' death on the cross meant that all his sins could be forgiven.

As I said before, this guy was very rough-looking and had numerous tattoos, as well as huge arms and shoulders from lifting weights, but he just started weeping in my front seat. I pulled the car over to the side of the road, and he told me he'd just gotten out of prison and had been there for a few years. How could God forgive him?

He asked me if God was going to mess around with him (not quite in that vocabulary) and play with his mind. Then, as he cried loudly, he asked me how and why God would love him.

I was in total awe once again that God had picked out this very day for this man to receive His love and forgiveness. The presence of God had filled the car, and both of us were overwhelmed. Yes, it was awkward, but somehow, we seemed to know it was going to be okay. God was moving upon both of us, and I put my hand on his shoulder and began to pray because, at that point, that's all I knew to do. Remember, this guy had just gotten out of prison, where you keep your hands to yourself if you want to stay healthy. But I just kept praying, and it was undeniable that God was filling this guy with His love and forgiveness.

I have learned to be as quiet as possible when God interrupts a life and to let God do the work through His Holy Spirit. The Bible tells us that we need to be led by the Holy Spirit and to rely on His power to accomplish things for God. *"'Not by might nor by power, but by My Spirit,' says the LORD of hosts"* (Zechariah 4:6). The tricky part is knowing what our role is, and that can be learned only by "on-the-job training." If you ask God to use you, then get ready, because He will keep bringing opportunities your way! He is the One who is working in us, and it's His desire to use us to bring others to Himself. Therefore, He will anoint you and guide you and use you every day, if you will only ask Him and yield to Him.

Preparation and desire are the keys. Again, if you will begin to study God's Word and learn what He says about His love for the lost, and then give people His Word and not yours, then you will see miracles happen often, right in front of your eyes. Yes, I said "often"!

The greatest of all miracles is when a sinner repents. After I prayed for the hitchhiker, asking God to keep him and protect him, I encouraged him and drove him where he needed to go. I prayed and believed that God would lead him to a church and get him plugged in right away, just as God had guided me after I first met Jesus by leading me to one of those Gideon New Testaments at the bus station when I was on my way to Marine Corps boot camp, and had begun to teach me His Word.

I know the parable of the sower and the four kinds of soil on which the seed fell. (See, for example, Matthew 13:3–9.) I am very aware that Satan will try to steal the seed of the Word of God from people who don't understand it. I've heard about the percentage of people who usually come forward to receive Christ at evangelistic crusades and the lower numbers of those who actually continue on in a relationship with God.

But 1 John 5:14–15 tells us this:

Now this is the confidence that we have in Him, that if we ask anything according to His will, He hears us. And if we know that He hears us, whatever we ask, we know that we have the petitions that we have asked of Him.

I know for certain that the perfect will of God for the hitchhiker I picked up would be for him to go on with God and become a disciple of Jesus, so I am trusting that God will do just that in his life.

One of the biggest problems in the church is that we get so paralyzed by fears and doubts and just plain, old-fashioned laziness that we don't even try to win souls to Christ or pray and ask God to use us for His glory. And I know that some people take the concept of "predestination" (God choosing those who will be saved) to the point where they don't ever talk to anyone about faith in Christ. In fact, I once heard someone remark, "I didn't know if they were one of God's chosen, so I didn't know if I should say anything." Again, we allow all these excuses to convince us to justify our apathy for the lost, and we almost never share Jesus with people. Yet, remember, *"Whoever calls on the name of the* LORD *shall be saved"* (Romans 10:13). Our job is to care about the people around us, and God will work out all the rest.

> Our job is to care about the people around us, and God will work out all the rest.

If we would just humble ourselves and ask Him to forgive us and then simply request that He use us, He would gladly put us in situations *today* where we can demonstrate His love to someone. Again, Jesus said, *"You did not choose Me, but I chose you and appointed you that you should go and bear fruit, and that your fruit should remain, that whatever you ask the Father in My name He may give you"* (John 15:16).

This is why Christ came into the world—to save sinners like us and to use all of us to bring others to

Himself. Even if we just encourage others with His love, it honors God, and He delights in that.

I know that not everyone is an evangelist, and not everyone will meet people like I met the hitchhiker. But I do know that you can invite your neighbor over for coffee, you can play golf with your coworkers, or you can simply become a friend to someone in need. Before you know it, people will notice something different about you and ask you about the hope you have within you. (See 1 Peter 3:15.) Then, you can begin to tell them in a natural way of your love for the Savior and how Jesus fills your heart daily with His love and peace. I promise you that if you take one step toward God, He will take two steps toward you and use you for His glory.

God did not make following Him a big mystery. It may not be easy, but it's not a mystery. His Word is pure, and He made it plain for us through His Holy Spirit. Again, yield yourself to the Holy Spirit daily, and He will teach you and guide you on your way.

Can you imagine what our churches and Bible studies would be like if we began to hear how people shared Christ with their neighbors and friends, and how these neighbors and friends accepted Jesus right at their kitchen tables or on the golf course? Why not us, and why not now? Go ahead and ask God to use you today to make faith come alive in someone's heart. You just might see the greatest of all miracles happen before your very eyes!

> Ask God to use you today to make faith come alive in someone's heart.

14

Secret Power in High Places

*"A man is what he is on his knees before
God, and nothing more."* [2]

I am glad my mother truly knew this truth: All power and authority in this world and the universe lie with God Almighty. Someone once said, "The thing you need the most to walk this life victoriously for God is the thing you will be tempted to do the least... pray." Prayer is the single most important practice of a Christian's life. Please take thirty seconds now and say a simple prayer like this: "Father God, in the name of Jesus, please bring me into a deep relationship with You. Help me to daily get alone with You and talk with You. Burn within me the desire to spend time with You."

This is what prayer is—spending time with our heavenly Father. He longs to use us for His glory and honor, and prayer is our preparation for this. It is our preparation for giving more of ourselves

---

[2] This statement by nineteenth-century evangelist Robert Murray M'Cheyne was often quoted by Isobel Maxim, my praying mother!

to Him and for receiving more from Him. We give God our praise and adoration, and we receive His strength and wisdom to accomplish His purposes for our lives.

Unrealized potential is generally due to a lack of preparation. To prepare without including prayer is to act in ignorance of whose power you are operating in. If you ask experienced Christians what they would have done differently in their lives, they will always answer, "I wish I would have prayed more. I wish my daily personal time with God would have been a priority in my life."

God wants to maximize the potential of your life, whether you are eighty-five, twenty-five, or fifteen. God wants to share things with you that will cause you to grow closer to Him. Prayer is the act of opening your mind and heart to His still, small voice. To His whisper, His leading, His prompting.

PERSONAL ACCESS TO GOD!

There are not sufficient words in any language to describe what an astounding miracle it is to have personal access to God—yes, God Himself. We do a terrible job when we tell people that they "need" to pray and spend time with God. We make it sound like an obligation! It's as if we have to pay homage, or as if it's some kind of duty we have to perform because God has saved us.

Prayer is not a duty; it's a joy and a privilege. The following are just a few things the Word says about fellowshipping with God in prayer and experiencing His presence:

He who dwells in the secret place of the Most High shall abide under the shadow of the Almighty. (Psalm 91:1)

My voice You shall hear in the morning, O LORD; in the morning I will direct it to You, and I will look up. (Psalm 5:3)

Evening and morning and at noon I will pray, and cry aloud, and He shall hear my voice. (Psalm 55:17)

I love the LORD, because He has heard my voice and my supplications. Because He has inclined His ear to me, therefore I will call upon Him as long as I live.
(Psalm 116:1–2)

Let my prayer be set before You as incense, the lifting up of my hands as the evening sacrifice. (Psalm 141:2)

Seeing then that we have a great High Priest who has passed through the heavens, Jesus the Son of God, let us hold fast our confession. For we do not have a High Priest who cannot sympathize with our weaknesses, but was in all points tempted as we are, yet without sin. Let us therefore come boldly to the throne of grace, that we may obtain mercy and find grace to help in time of need. (Hebrews 4:14–16)

[Jesus said,] *If you abide in Me, and My words abide in you, you will ask what you desire, and it shall be done for you.*

(John 15:7)

Now this is the confidence that we have in Him [Jesus], that if we ask anything according to His will, He hears us. And if we know that He hears us, whatever we ask, we know that we have the petitions that we have asked of Him. (1 John 5:14–15)

If any of you lacks wisdom, let him ask of God, who gives to all liberally and without reproach, and it will be given to him. But let him ask in faith, with no doubting, for he who doubts is like a wave of the sea driven and tossed by the wind. For let not that man suppose that he will receive anything from the Lord; he is a double-minded man, unstable in all his ways. (James 1:5–8)

[Jesus said,] *And whatever you ask in My name, that I will do, that the Father may be glorified in the Son. If you ask anything in My name, I will do it.* (John 14:13–14)

[Jesus said,] *Therefore I say to you, whatever things you ask when you pray, believe that you receive them, and you will have them.* (Mark 11:24)

When you read these Scriptures, you can plainly see that God wants us to come to Him and spend time with Him. He also wants us to ask Him for the things that are on our hearts, and He wants to give us what we ask of Him. He already knows what is on our hearts and what we are thinking, so He wants to have a conversation with us about those things. God wants us to desire to meet with Him, to be excited about being together with Him. He longs for us to come into His presence and talk with Him. He is our heavenly Father. He created us; He formed us out of the dust of the earth. (See Genesis 2:7.) He knew us while we were in our mothers' wombs. (See, for example, Jeremiah 1:4–5; Psalm 139:13–16.) He says we are *"fearfully and wonderfully made"* (Psalm 139:14). He knows every part of our beings. He knows our strengths, our weaknesses, our fears, our hopes, and our dreams. He knows what we truly long to be like, and *He* wants to help us with all these things— if we will only let Him!

> God knows our strengths, our weaknesses, our fears, our hopes, and our dreams, and He wants to help us with all these things.

Coming to Him and having a conversation with Him *is* prayer. Don't allow other ideas about prayer— for example, that it is "burdensome" or "boring"—to stop you from beginning today to spend time with God your Father. He is almighty God, and He wants to talk with you every day. He doesn't mind if you have to ask over and over again for His help with something. And it doesn't matter what is on your mind. Again, He already knows about it, He has the power to fix anything, and He longs to give you the desires of your heart.

No, He is not going to be an "errand boy" for you and answer requests that are not good for you. Remember that Jesus said, *"If you abide in Me, and*

My words abide in you, you will ask what you desire, and it shall be done for you" (John 15:7). The key here is *"if you abide in Me."* The reason Jesus prefaced His statement in that way is simple: If you are abiding in Him, and His words are abiding in you, you are not going to be asking for things that won't be beneficial for you and the others around you. Just as any good parents will not give their children things that they *know* would hurt them, God will not give us things that would hurt us in some way.

Can we know the will of God before we ask Him for something in prayer? The simple answer is yes, but, at times, we get our own desires mixed up with His desires for us. You must remember that God is your loving Father, and He wants to bless you and see you grow into the man or woman He longs for you to become. Therefore, you can trust Him to guide you even in your prayers.

> *Likewise the Spirit also helps in our weaknesses. For we do not know what we should pray for as we ought, but the Spirit Himself makes intercession for us with groanings which cannot be uttered. Now He who searches the hearts knows what the mind of the Spirit is, because He makes intercession for the saints according to the will of God.* (Romans 8:26–27)

When we don't know how to pray in a certain situation, the Holy Spirit will teach us, if we will only yield ourselves to Him.

You can see that it is an awesome privilege for us to have access to God Himself, to start our times with Him expressing thankfulness, to be able to worship and adore Him, and to be aware that He is God and we are His children and that He will take care of us. We can trust Him; we can bless Him; we can admire Him; we can honor Him.

By having the right heart attitude and an understanding of prayer, we can enter into the presence of our Father, who can do anything. Yes, He can do anything! When we truly comprehend that reality, it changes our awareness; our spiritual eyes and understanding are opened to the true privilege we have. When we recognize our prerogative in prayer, our opportunity to go to God becomes a joy, and we can't wait to be with Him. And the really awesome thing is this: He can't wait for us to get there! We can have a very close relationship with God Almighty. Then, the quote "A man is what he is on his knees before God, and nothing more" becomes so clear.

Prayer Is a Weapon for War!

Prayer is also a weapon of power in the spiritual world. That's right—a weapon of power. Are you surprised? In the New Testament, at the end of the passage where the apostle Paul talked about spiritual warfare and the armor of God, he included prayer as an element of spiritual warfare, encouraging us to be *"praying always with all prayer and supplication in the Spirit"* (Ephesians 6:18).

Remember how I related that, on the night of my accident, the devil's voice was taunting my mother, asking her where her mighty God was right at that moment? When she got home and started crying out to the Lord, the Holy Spirit reminded her to have faith, because God cannot fail! As my mother prayed for me, she was actually battling for my soul and my healing. Of course, I was totally unaware of what was going on. But my mother was bringing me before the throne of God in prayer and crying out for His mercy and grace.

Second Timothy 2:26 says, *"That they may come to their senses and escape the snare of the devil, having been taken captive by him to do his will."* Think about this for a minute: the devil has taken some people captive to do his will! If he has the power to take people captive to do his will, who will rescue them? How will they be set free?

Do you know anyone who fits this description? Do you have a loved one in this situation? Is there someone at work you know who is bound by Satan? It doesn't matter to God how ignorant or addicted or bound up a person is; He has given us the power of prayer to release this person from the prison of Satan. Whether or not it happens visually, as it did for me, the reality is that Jesus Christ will walk into the midst of the misery that person is living in, look into his eyes, and tell him He loves him. He will reach out His hand and pick him up from the pit he is in. Jesus will hear the cries of your heart in prayer and respond to you, too. You will act as the bridge to move this person into the presence of God!

Jesus is not afraid to walk right into the depths of hell and look Satan in the face and say, "Get your hands off of him right now. This person belongs to Me!" Absolutely nothing is impossible for God. He longs to reconcile sinners to Himself. He longs to walk into the most impossible prisons of sin and to release the prisoners from their captivity. And He allows us to have a part in their salvation through prayer!

I believe that God is glorified most when a sinner looks up to Him and cries to be set free. I am not just talking about someone who is addicted to drugs or alcohol. It could be the gentlest, kindest person you have ever met; yet, when that person asks Jesus to cleanse him and forgive him for his sins (since we all sin), the same things happen to him, as well. He is forgiven and cleansed by the blood of Christ. He is born again and becomes a child of God. The Bible says the angels in heaven *rejoice* when one sinner repents. (See Luke 15:10 NIV.) Yes, they have a party in heaven; how cool is that? We can have a huge part in bringing people to the party through prayer.

"Who Is Praying for You?"

I received a phone call from a businessman who had recently moved to Philadelphia and had been given my name by one of his friends. He called me to discuss some business opportunities, and I agreed to meet with him in my office, but only reluctantly, because I had heard about "the latest and greatest widgets" so many times before that I didn't expect much. Little did I know that this man had played professional football in the NFL, and when he walked into my office, believe me, he looked like it! He was massive. His upper body looked like the Incredible Hulk. And his name was Louis.

We shook hands and started talking, and I asked him how he'd gotten my name and number. He had given me this information on the phone when he'd called, but I didn't remember. After he sat down, it dawned on me who had referred him to me; it was a Christian businessman I knew.

> All of a sudden, the presence of God started filling the room mightily. You didn't have to be a genius to realize that God wanted this man.

We started talking about business for a minute or two, and then, all of a sudden, the presence of God started filling the room mightily. (Remember that almost every day, I ask the Lord to guide me and use me to make faith come alive in somebody's heart. Doing this helps me to be sensitive to God's Spirit.) I don't remember having said anything to him about God or anything along those lines. Maybe he'd seen the small Bible on my desk, or maybe something else had triggered it, but this very athletic-looking, ex-NFL football player sitting across the desk from me began squirming in his seat. And then he started weeping!

Well, you didn't have to be a genius to realize that God wanted this man, and so I began trying to figure out who was praying for him. I handed him a box of Kleenex, and he was feeling very uncomfortable and telling me that he didn't know what was happening. I didn't know exactly what God was doing, and, at the same time, I couldn't wait to hear who was praying for him and to listen to the testimony that was about to unfold before me. I was thinking of all the other times something similar had happened, and, again, it's always exciting to watch it occur, but this guy was pretty big, and he was visibly shaken and upset, as if he wondered if I had some kind of a "voodoo thing" going on.

I looked over at him and asked, *"Who is praying for you?"* Then, in a second, he realized what I meant, and he started crying profusely. I just kept giving him Kleenex and watching the power of God minister to him.

He said this never happened to him and asked, "What's going on?"

God's presence was so undeniable by that point that I told him he was a marked man! I said that whoever was praying for him was in intercession before God for his soul and that God was answering their prayers.

He then revealed that his wife and his mother had been telling him he needed to get right with God and surrender his life to Jesus.

I marveled at the mercy of God in bringing this man to my office, and at the fact that the first time I met him, God had shown up and totally overwhelmed him with His presence because He loved him so much and was reaching out to him.

Maybe it was because I was a businessman myself, whom he would listen to, that God decided to use me to share the gospel with him. Maybe God knew that something destructive was about to take place in his life, and He wanted to stop it from happening. I didn't know, but I did know that God had ordained this moment in time for him to come to Christ, and that, if he would listen, the God who created the entire universe would step out of heaven and right into his life!

I shared the gospel with him (that Jesus came to earth, died for the sins of humanity, rose from the grave, and is coming again). He just sat there weeping, and then he started asking Jesus to cleanse him and forgive him. He knew now that the presence in the room was God and that He was there for him this very special day.

I kept sharing the Scriptures with him, and, deep in his heart, he knew that God was calling him to come home. He knew he had been running from God. He knew his wife and mother had been praying for him, so that what was happening to him began to make perfect sense.

We both were in total awe of what was transpiring, and I was so thankful and deeply touched once again to watch God bring someone to Himself. It's always like a 3-D movie for me when this happens. Although I am a part of all that is occurring, it's still as if I'm watching it unfold from a seat in a theater balcony, seeing the love of God touch someone that dramatically and bring him to the Lord in such a real way, and it almost always takes me back to the day Jesus came to me.

I will never forget it. I can see it like it was yesterday. And I remember when my dad took me to the church on the way home from the hospital late at night. I remember walking down the center aisle with all of the lights off, looking up at the cross, and saying to Jesus that I didn't understand all that had happened and that I was going to need His help to make it. I pray to God that the reverent feeling that seems to burn within me every time He places someone in front of me for the purpose of salvation never stops. I want it to be there every day.

Louis and I went to lunch right after our meeting in my office. He sensed that God had interrupted his life, and he knew he would never be the same. After lunch, I prayed for him, asking that God would guide him and his wife to a great church where they would get involved right away.

I stayed in touch with Louis, and Cathy and I later drove up to meet him and his wife, and they invited us to the church they attended. God had indeed placed them in a good church.

The idea that God is actively seeking people to bring them to salvation is almost incomprehensible unless you look at it in the light of the gospel. The Bible says, *"The Lord is...not willing that any should perish but that **all** should come to repentance"* (2 Peter 3:9, emphasis added).

What a privilege it is to be used by God in this incredibly awesome adventure!

> If you have been running away from God and His will for you, ask Him to make Himself real to you.

Since you are reading this book right now, I can promise you that God is speaking to you in some way. If you are like Louis was and have been running away from God and His will for you, would you please consider pausing right now and asking God to make Himself real to you? Ask Him if what Jim is saying here has any truth to it at all. Ask Him to reveal Himself to you and to open your eyes to humanity's greatest truth, that Jesus Christ is the Savior of the world. God loves you with an everlasting love and desires to walk with you. Won't you bow your heart to Him and let Him?

FINDING A WAY TO JESUS

If you are already a believer, don't ignore the power you have to bring your loved ones before the Lord in prayer. When we love people and want the best for them, we will go to great lengths to help them. The following is my favorite Bible account that illustrates the help we can give in bringing others to Jesus.

> *Now it happened on a certain day, as He* [Jesus] *was teaching, that there were Pharisees and teachers of the law sitting by, who had come out of every town of Galilee, Judea, and Jerusalem. And the power of the Lord was present to heal them. Then behold, men brought on a bed a man who was paralyzed, whom they sought to bring in and lay before Him. And when they could not find how they might bring him in, because of the crowd, they went up on the housetop and let him down with his bed through the tiling into the midst before Jesus.* [In other words, for the sake of their friend, they tore the roof off to get to Jesus!] *When He saw their faith, He said to him, "Man, your sins are forgiven you." And the scribes and the Pharisees began to reason, saying, "Who is this who speaks blasphemies? Who can forgive sins but God alone?" But when Jesus perceived their thoughts, He answered and said to them, "Why are you reasoning in your hearts? Which is easier, to say, 'Your sins are forgiven you,' or to say, 'Rise up and walk'? But that you may know that the Son of Man has power on earth to forgive*

sins"; He said to the man who was para-
lyzed, "I say to you, arise, take up your bed,
and go to your house." Immediately he rose
up before them, took up what he had been
lying on, and departed to his own house,
glorifying God. And they were all amazed,
and they glorified God and were filled with
fear, saying, "We have seen strange things
today!"   (Luke 5:17–26)

"Strange things"—unusual things—God things! The guys in the above story were pretty bold! They tore a hole in someone's roof to get to Jesus. Maybe the owner of that house was a stranger, but they knew that they had to get to Jesus!

My mother did something very similar the night of my accident so long ago. In prayer, she tore off a hole in the roof, and she lowered me down to Jesus! She knew He could heal—and that He would heal— so she boldly brought me before Him.

She would not give up. Satan had me captive, bound in his prison, and she would not leave me there, no matter what I did. A mother's love is something so compelling and intense; it is a small picture of the love that God has for all humanity. God sent His Son to earth to release all of us from the prison of sin.

I want to ask you again: Do you have a loved one who is in a hellish prison right now? Or, does Satan have you locked in a prison cell of sin? Has Satan been lying to you, telling you that there is no way out: "You'll be here forever; others may be set free, but not you"?

Stop the lies right now! Praying, crying out to God, will set you or your loved one free. We can tear open the roof of that prison through prayer. Praying with faith, based on the Word of God, is the way to lower a loved one into the presence of Jesus Christ. Jesus is standing right outside the prison cell. He longs to touch you or your loved one and set you free.

God's perfect plan is to reconcile the world to Himself. When we pray for people to get saved, we are in the center of God's perfect will, and He will move heaven and earth to reach them. No matter what situation a person is in, His power is limitless. Nothing can stop the hand of God from reaching out to someone. Nothing or no one can stop God!

> Keep praying and believing; don't stop, no matter what. Don't listen to the lies of Satan. God answers prayer.

Keep praying and believing; don't stop, no matter what. Don't listen to the lies of Satan. God answers prayer. Read that statement again—*God answers prayer.* He delights in forgiving. He delights in bringing sinners to Himself to love them and cleanse them.

Prayer is the answer for your loved ones who desperately need miracles in their lives. Even when the people you pray for have no clue what you are doing for them, they can be set free by your intercession. God is the power that changes people's lives, just as He changed yours and mine!

15

CLIMBING THE HEIGHTS OF SHARING CHRIST

The hardest part of Christianity is living it out. It's one thing to "talk big" about God; it's completely different to "live big" for God. It's the ultimate aim of a Christian's life; however, we cannot do it on our own. No matter how much money we possess, no matter how many degrees we earn, no matter how much fame we have, we must rely upon the power of the Holy Spirit living within us. God knows my make-up because He created me, and He knows all of my tendencies, especially when I think, *Okay, now I've got it—I can do this thing. Come on, God, we'll show them!* That is my pride, and it's a recipe for disaster!

LIVING IT OUT

One thing all Christians have in common is our "wandering hearts," which can lead us away from the Lord. That is why you need the Holy Spirit to walk with you daily, to guide you, to protect you, and to speak to your heart and mind. He will put strong impressions on you, as if they were coming from a well deep inside of you. As I wrote earlier, you will learn to be sensitive to this "voice" from within you the more time you spend studying God's Word and the more time you spend in prayer with Him.

God longs to communicate with us for many reasons, but, primarily, He wants to love us, encourage us, and teach us more about Himself. His main desire is that we understand how He loved us so much that He sent His Son to die for us. Now, He wants us to share that love with all the people to whom He prompts us to speak by the Holy Spirit. Let me tell you about another experience I had with the Holy Spirit's leading in this way.

I boarded a flight going from Kenya to South Africa and found myself sitting next to a woman who had just finished climbing Mt. Kilimanjaro! Her eyes blazing with excitement, she began telling me all about her climb. She had such a sense of wonder from her challenging adventure that she couldn't keep quiet. She was bursting to relate her experiences and her sense of great accomplishment. Her enthusiasm was contagious, and I gave her my undivided attention so I could share in her joy and hear her amazing story.

What she didn't know was, that morning, and then again right before the flight, I had prayed and asked the Lord to help me be sensitive to the people around me, to use me to make faith come alive in someone's heart that day. Now I was "stuck" beside this young woman for the four-hour flight. She was so friendly and wanted to talk about her climbing, so I prayed that the Lord would help me share His love with her before the flight was over. I knew how important it was to wait for the Holy Spirit to speak to my heart, to tell me what to say and how to share God's love with her.

I listened to the amazing climbing stories for about an hour. It really was exciting to hear her describe the rigorous challenges they had encountered during the climb, as well as the magnificent beauty of the mountain. All the while, I wondered, *How can I share with her the most exciting truth that has ever been told to humanity?* I was also silently asking the Holy Spirit how I could turn the conversation to God in a way that would minister specifically to her. Just then, it became as clear as day to me! I was really excited, because I knew it was the perfect approach for her. It had to be on a large scale, just like the story she was sharing with me.

> I wondered, *How can I share with her the most exciting truth that has ever been told to humanity?*

This is how I started: As she continued telling me her story, I asked her many questions along the way. When she came to the end, I exclaimed, "That was just incredible! I can only imagine one other experience that would be even greater than climbing Mt. Kilimanjaro!"

She sat back in her seat and asked me, wide-eyed, "What in the world could that be?" I answered her joyfully, "I can introduce you to the God who *created* that glorious mountain! I want to share with you how much that God loves you and wants to have a personal relationship with you." She listened intently as I assured her that the joy she had experienced in that climb could be magnified a million times over if she personally knew the God who wanted to have an intimate relationship with her.

I shared how God had sent His own Son, Jesus, down to earth to die for sinners like her and like me, and how He longs for us to come and talk with Him. When I told her that God wants to spend time with us and to reveal Himself as we seek Him, she began to cry. She started to experience His presence right there on that plane.

Perhaps she was thinking about some of the natural beauty she'd seen in His creation on that mountain, or maybe she was thinking about how awesome it was that the One who had created the mountain in the first place was interested in her. Maybe she'd had an experience with God years earlier. I wasn't sure, but I reassured her that it was no coincidence we'd been seated together on that flight.

I shared with her, "This very morning, before I got on the plane, I prayed a simple prayer that God would lead me to someone who needed to know Him. As I sit here with you, you know that this God who created Mt. Kilimanjaro is knocking on the door of your heart, longing to have a personal relationship with you."

Although I probably will never see her again, I told her to ask God to reveal Himself to her personally. Normally, I would ask the person I am sharing with if he or she would like to pray and receive Christ as Savior right then, but this time was a little different. She was crying, and the plane was landing, so I told her to just pray in the quietness of her own time and to ask the Lord into her life. I said that I would be praying for her. As you read this, I am still praying for her, even though I don't know where she is or what she is doing.

The point of this story is that God wants all of us to be sensitive to His Holy Spirit, who lives within us and desires to use us to bring others to Himself. God longs for us to tell others about His love for them. When we rely on God the Holy Spirit, He will place us in situations where His power in us will bring love, hope, and encouragement to others. Remember that the Holy Spirit is our Teacher, and all we have to do is yield ourselves to Him in the study of God's Word, and He will teach us all things about God the Father, Jesus, and Himself.

> When we rely on the Holy Spirit, He will place us in situations where His power in us will bring love, hope, and encouragement to others.

LEARNING TO BE SENSITIVE TO GOD'S SPIRIT

Our responsibility and privilege is to learn how we can be more sensitive to God's Holy Spirit. Then, we can share God's love everywhere we go—*through Him*, not in our own power or with our own words.

In my early years of being a Christian, I was not very good at waiting on God for much of anything because of the thankfulness I had in my heart toward Him for saving me. In my zeal, I often just shared my faith everywhere I went, regardless of whether people wanted to hear it. Looking back, I realize I must have offended a lot of people because of my ignorance about the guidance of the Holy Spirit. My desire had been for them to experience the love of God Almighty in their lives and to begin the journey of allowing Him to love them and be with them the same way He had been with me. I know that sounds like a good desire, and it is, but I soon realized that not everyone shared the same beliefs I did, and, in fact, many people were really upset with me for trying to "push" my beliefs on them. Not everyone was interested in learning about God's love for him or her.

Wow, was that an eye-opener! Some people would actually get very mad at me and say things like, "Hey, Maxim, if you need that Jesus stuff as a crutch, fine; just keep it to yourself!"

Jesus said, *"No one can come to Me unless the Father who sent Me draws him"* (John 6:44). In other words, we need to ask God to lead us daily to those with whom He would have us share our faith, and we must be led by the Holy Spirit whenever we do so. Even when it was the leading of God's Spirit for me to share the story of how Jesus died for our sins, there have been many times when people have gotten downright belligerent with me for thinking I had the right to tell them that Jesus Christ is the way God has provided for us to spend eternity with Him.

I have had some really tough arguments with people, even though that was the last thing in the world I wanted; it just happened. What is the answer to this dilemma?

GOD LIVING HIS LIFE THROUGH US!

God's plan is for us to yield our lives to Him so that *He can live His life through us.* People need to *know* about the God who is living inside us. When we yield ourselves to the power of God within us— the Holy Spirit—we become God's agents of change for those around us. He really will work in us and through us to bless and encourage others. It is the power of God's Spirit showing through us that causes people to hunger for what we have found, and it is God working through us that changes lives. So, it's not about us; it's all about Him. He changes others' lives just as He changed ours.

This is one of my daily prayers, and you may want to consider praying something like this yourself:

> Father God, in the name of Jesus, I come before You and ask that You would fill me again with Your Spirit. Father, I ask that You would let a fresh anointing come upon me today to serve You. Please use me today to make faith come alive in someone's heart.

When we focus on God's power living within us and ask for His power to be used to bless and help other people, we stop focusing on ourselves. We start living big in God's eyes by being concerned about the people around us and not just our own needs.

The Holy Spirit wants to have close fellowship with us. He wants us to grow in our understanding and knowledge of Him. He wants us to yield ourselves to Him and to be sensitive to how He desires to use us in every situation. And He wants our outreach to others to be a true adventure in Him!

16

BE A GIVER

In life, there are givers and there are takers. There are sustainers and there are drainers. The way you can become a giver, or sustainer—a blessing to others—is by *knowing and believing God's Word.*

Knowing God intimately means knowing His Word. This is what the apostle Paul said shortly before he was executed for his faith: *"Be diligent to present yourself approved to God, a worker who does not need to be ashamed, **rightly dividing the word of truth"** (2 Timothy 2:15, emphasis added).*

Paul was a man whom God had to literally knock off his feet to get his attention. His conversion is described in the Bible, in the book of Acts, chapter 9. He was a man who hated Christians and went out of his way to kill anyone who claimed to love Jesus, including women and children. But, after he met the living Christ, he became a "vessel of honor" in God's hands (see verses 19–21), and God used him to write about half of the New Testament. Never think that you cannot be used mightily because of your past—whatever it is. The Bible plainly tells us that when we are born again, *"if anyone is in Christ, he is a new creation; old things have passed away; behold, all things have become new"* (2 Corinthians 5:17).

The Lord prepares us in different ways to be used by Him. One way of preparation is to be taught by more mature believers in the Lord. Paul had a young disciple in the Lord by the name of Timothy, and he wrote two letters to Timothy that can be found in the New Testament. The second letter was written from a cold, dark jail cell in Rome, where Paul had been imprisoned. This letter is full of tremendous advice on how to live a God-honoring life as a *"good soldier of Jesus Christ"* (2 Timothy 2:3).

Paul knew that he would shortly be killed for his faith in Christ. What he shared with Timothy were some of his last words on this earth. From Paul's point of view, these were the most important things that he wanted to pass on to his young disciple.

Paul reminded Timothy, *"God has not given us a spirit of fear, but of power and of love and of a sound mind. Therefore do not be ashamed of the testimony of our Lord"* (2 Timothy 1:7–8). He encouraged him, *"Be strong in the grace that is in Christ Jesus. And the things that you have heard from me among many witnesses, commit these to faithful men who will be able to teach others also"* (2:1–2). Knowing the temptations of the world, Paul reminded him, *"Flee also youthful lusts; but pursue righteousness, faith, love, peace with those who call on the Lord out of a pure heart. But avoid foolish and ignorant disputes, knowing that they generate strife"* (2:22–23).

Read all of 1 and 2 Timothy when you have the opportunity. Please pay special attention to these words of Paul, as they will help you to grow deeply in your faith and walk with God. You will be able to teach these truths to other believers wherever you go. Paul constantly encouraged Timothy to study the Scriptures to make sure he would be ready and qualified for ministry and to have the necessary knowledge of God's Word to share with others.

Be Available to Learn

It's up to each one of us to be available for God to teach us. There is no better way for a new believer to learn than to start studying the Bible right now. I have found that the best way to *initially* study the Bible is according to topic, so that you can memorize Scriptures pertaining to certain subjects. If you are just starting your faith journey, knowing what God says about various topics that come up in conversation will enable you to be more confident in sharing your newfound faith in Christ. Hopefully, this will encourage you to continue to share it more and more.

After you have spent some time studying these topics and asking the Holy Spirit to help you commit relevant verses to memory, you can be sure that He will open up opportunities for you to share and will "nudge" you to take a step of faith and begin telling others what you have learned. It's really awesome when you sense the Holy Spirit leading you to the people in your path who need to hear about God's love.

Don't be surprised when the most "unlikely" people—people whom you previously thought would laugh at you or have no interest in God whatsoever—stand there totally focused on what you are sharing. They may not want to pray with you that day, but you can just keep loving them and giving them what God says in His Word—not just what *you* think! Stay focused on what you have learned from His Word.

For example, let's take a look at the topic of salvation. In the back of many Bibles, there is a concordance, or a directory of words. If you look up a particular keyword, you will find a list of references where that word can be found in the Bible. In the concordance section of my Bible, under the word *salvation*, there are approximately thirty Scripture references that I could look up to see what God says about salvation. When I study like this, certain Scriptures seem to stand out to me a little more than others. I write those particular Scripture passages down on three-by-five cards and carry them with me throughout the day. From time to time, I reread these Scriptures, committing them to memory. Then, I ask the Holy Spirit to give me an opportunity to share my faith with someone that day. He will certainly guide me to someone in order to share God's love with that person in some way, perhaps even to talk to him or her about one of the Scriptures I have been studying.

> The Holy Spirit is so faithful; He will help you to memorize Scriptures and recall them when it's time to share them with others.

Therefore, ask the Holy Spirit to help you to memorize some of these verses, as well. Then, the next time you meet an old friend or sit next to someone on a bus or at the airport, you will recall these Scriptures to share with that person. The Holy Spirit is so faithful; He will help you to memorize the Scriptures and recall them when it's time to share them with others. He wants to see hurting people come into the kingdom of God even more than you do, and He will help you to become a soulwinner, if you will only ask Him.

THE GREATEST THEOLOGICAL TRUTH

We had a major snowfall one winter that totaled about twenty-six inches, and I had a four-wheel-drive vehicle, so I thought I would go out early and take a ride in the fresh snow. I had finished clearing off all the snow from my SUV, and I was about to get in and back out of my driveway, when I saw a man walking down the street. I wondered who it was and why someone would be out walking in this blizzard. As I backed out of my driveway, I recognized the man as one of my neighbors, so I lowered the front passenger-side window and asked him if I could help in any way.

He said he had to get to work, so I told him to please get in, and I would be glad to drive him. I knew he was employed by a government contractor and was working on some sensitive or classified projects. We were the only ones on the road, and although he'd never told me what his work was, precisely, he'd said enough that I realized it had to be very important for him to need to be out walking in this terrible weather to get to his job that morning.

As soon as he stepped into my vehicle—even before he was fully seated—he looked over at me and asked, "Why do you send your kids to Christian school when you know our township has some of the best schools in the country?" I knew that John had two Ph.D.'s and was one of those off-the-charts intelligent people, and so were his kids. One day, I'd been fixing a ceiling fan in my kitchen, and one of his boys had been at my home playing with one of my sons. The two boys had been coming through the kitchen when the man's son had stopped and started to enlighten me on the correct way to wire this particular fan and about the electrical circuits involved with this type of appliance! Of course, I acted as if I knew exactly what he was discussing with me. I nodded to him and then told him my son was calling him from the other room and needed him for something. This young man was often asked by the school to help whenever their computers gave them any kind of problems, so you can imagine the type of intellect his father had as a mathematical genius with two Ph.D.'s.

Well, I knew that a simple hello was not going to happen, but I also knew that this was definitely a God moment. So, I said one of those millisecond prayers, and I instantly knew how to reply. I looked over at him and said, "John, I don't want my children to be sheltered in any way from the truth, so that's why." I could see a look come over him that showed he just didn't know how to reply to that, even as smart as he was. He just grimaced and asked, "What in the world are you talking about?"

The reason I ask God every day to make me sensitive to those around me, so that I can share His love with them, is that I want to be sure I am thinking about God's agenda for them and not my own. As I mentioned before, I have tried to thump people over the head with the Bible, but that leads only to my trying to get *my* agenda across and not God's. With that attitude, I would just be witnessing to witness and not truly concerned for the person I was speaking with. But when I honestly want to talk with people about how much God loves them, a great percentage of the time, I can at least have a dialogue with someone who is genuine. The result may not be that the person ends up asking God to cleanse him and forgive him, but the seed of God's Word has been planted, and He will water that seed the way He wants to.

> I ask God to make me sensitive to others so I can share His love with them and focus on His agenda rather than my own.

So, just as this man finished asking, "What in the world are you talking about?" I looked him right in the eye and said, "Do you think that my children are going to hear in public school that Jesus Christ died for their sins and the sins of mankind, and that God Almighty wants to walk with them daily and be their God, and that they can be His children? The Bible tells us in John 3:16 that God so loved the world that He gave His only begotten Son, that whosoever believes in Him can spend eternity with God and walk with Him in heaven. The Bible tells us in 1 Timothy 2:3–4 that it is God's desire that all men come to the knowledge of the truth. Do you want the truth to be hidden from you?"

This man was trained as a scientist and needed proof that something existed, not just the talk of a well-intentioned Christian who thought he knew enough about the God of the universe to convince him—while sitting in a vehicle during a huge snowstorm—that God loved Him. So, he started debating

me with all the typical questions that most intel-
lectuals want to discuss when confronted with any
philosophy that may be foreign to them, not just the
gospel. He challenged me by asking how any loving
God could allow children to go hungry. Then, he said
that if my God had all this power, why did people
all over the world have to suffer with different types
of diseases? Then, his question was, how could I sit
there and tell him that the Bible was a book that was
God-inspired and that God gave the men who wrote
it the words to write, and that those words were the
absolute answers to all of our questions?

Well, I gave him as many Scriptures as I could
on those issues and tried to stay on point with them,
because I knew that, given how smart he was, I needed all the help I could get. For example, I explained to
him that it is God's enemy, Satan, and not God, who
causes the suffering in the world, and that Jesus said
in John 10:10, *"The thief does not come except to steal,
and to kill, and to destroy. I have come that they may
have life, and that they may have it more abundantly."*
That Jesus described His ministry in this way:

> *The Spirit of the LORD is upon Me, because
> He has anointed Me to preach the gospel to
> the poor; He has sent Me to heal the bro-
> kenhearted, to proclaim liberty to the cap-
> tives and recovery of sight to the blind, to
> set at liberty those who are oppressed.*
> (Luke 4:18)

I told him that God promises to eliminate all
sorrow, pain, and death when Christ returns (see
Revelation 21:4), and that those who come to Christ
become His "body" and are to do, through Him, the

same things He did when He lived on the earth—bring hope and healing to those who are hurting. (See Matthew 10:7–8; Matthew 25:31–46.) I explained that both the Old and New Testament affirm the wisdom of living according to God's Word in order to experience true life and peace (see, for example, Joshua 1:7–8; Proverbs 1:1–7; Matthew 4:4; 2 Timothy 3:16–17), and that faith in God is not blind but reflects *"substance"* and *"evidence"* in the spiritual realm, which is the ultimate reality but cannot be seen with the physical eyes (see, for example, Psalm 33:6; Hebrews 11:1–3).

After discussing these things for a while, I realized that, even though this man was hearing the truth, God had to open his eyes, because all the debating in the world was not going to win him to the living Christ that I knew. The Bible says in John 6:44 that no one comes to Christ unless the Father draws that person to Him. Obviously, I'd been praying as we were discussing all these issues, and I was at the end of what I knew to share with him. Then, finally, I knew just what to say, and I had no idea what was about to happen.

I looked at him and said, "John, the greatest theological truth in all the world that has ever been taught to mankind is this…." His eyes were riveted on me, as if to say, *Please, let this be right. I hope what Jim is about to tell me is true.* I continued, "That truth is this: *'Jesus loves me! This I know, for the Bible tells me so.'*" Then, I asked him, since he was a mathematical genius, "What are the odds that I would be backing out of my driveway at the precise moment you were walking down the street, and that our paths would meet at that spot on the earth today?"

I just kept looking into his eyes, and then, right in front of me, this intellectual giant began to weep before the God of the universe. He had come to the end of himself and found out that his heavenly Father was waiting there patiently for him to come home. He told me that he just wanted to have some rest. He just wanted to have some peace. He said that, yes, he was very educated, but that, in many ways, it had been a curse to him and not a blessing. I told him that God would use all of it for His glory from now on, and that it could be a huge blessing to many people. I asked him if he wanted to receive Jesus Christ into his life right now, and he said yes. So, we prayed, and he asked for forgiveness for his sins, including pride, and he said that he wanted God to take the reins of his life. He had become like a little child, just as the Bible says we need to. (See Matthew 18:3.)

I dropped John off at work, and we agreed to meet for lunch that day. We had a time of discussing just what had happened in my vehicle, and it was obvious that the peace of God was resting upon him. I knew of a church that some of his coworkers attended, and I tried to seek them out, tell them about John's conversion, and ask if they would invite him to their Bible studies and begin to have fellowship with him. I knew that God would make a way for him to grow in his faith. God is faithful to His Word above all things, and I knew I could trust Him to take care of John.

I was so humbled to be with my neighbor the day God interrupted his life and brought him home. I was in complete awe to realize how God had caused me to back out of my driveway during the twenty-six-inch snowstorm at the precise moment John was walking down the street. Can you understand now why it is so important to ask God to use you today to make faith come alive in somebody's heart? Can you understand why we need to prepare ourselves to share our faith with others? Can you begin to understand God's heart a little better? God loved the world so much that He gave His only Son, so that *whoever* calls upon His name will be saved.

I know that the testimonies I've been sharing in this book are not like the "usual" ones in which you share your faith with a coworker, friend, or relative, and that person wants to pray with you to receive Christ. I have also had those kinds of experiences, and they are just as beautiful and as meaningful to almighty God as when the apostle Paul was knocked off his horse and surrendered to Jesus. But I wanted to share these particular ones to show you that nobody is beyond God's reach and that God longs to use you as His instrument to bring others home. If you ask God to use you today to make faith come alive in someone, get ready for a great adventure of faith!

> You may not have the gift of evangelism, but you can develop a greater awareness of the Holy Spirit leading you and nudging you to take a step of faith.

WHY DON'T WE SHARE CHRIST WITH OTHERS?

Most Christians do not share their faith and lead people to Jesus simply because they have never memorized any Scripture or desired to be used by the Holy Spirit. Other times, they are simply afraid of the possible rejection. So often, I hear the excuse, "I don't have the gift of evangelism like you do, so I have never (or have not often) shared my faith with people." Well, again, you may not have the gift of evangelism like Billy Graham, but you can develop a greater awareness of and sensitivity to the Holy Spirit leading you, guiding you, and nudging you to take a step of faith. Then, you can simply tell someone how Jesus saved you and cleansed you of your sin, and how He lives in your heart. Wouldn't it be great to allow the Lord to flow through you into someone else's life and then watch that person progress in his or her faith journey with God?

Paul wrote this in his first letter to the Christians in the city of Corinth:

> *Do you not know that those who run in a race all run, but one receives the prize? Run in such a way that you may obtain it. And everyone who competes for the prize is temperate in all things. Now they do it to obtain a perishable crown, but we for an imperishable crown. Therefore I run thus: not with uncertainty. Thus I fight: not as one who beats the air. But I discipline my body and bring it into subjection, lest, when I have preached to others, I myself should become disqualified.* (1 Corinthians 9:24–27)

No More Excuses!

Please, do not make excuses for not studying the Bible! Maybe God will call you to be a pastor or teacher of His Word. Maybe He will call you to be in the marketplace as a businessperson. Wherever He calls you, you can be sure He has called you to tell others about Him, and you cannot do it with excellence unless you know the Word of God.

You can study on your own, and you can also find excellent Bible study guides to work through. In addition, join a good Bible study with committed believers. And, most important, find a good Bible-believing and Bible-teaching church and get involved. Introduce yourself to the pastor and tell him you will commit yourself to pray for him and his family.

I have a promise for you: *If you will* develop a heart attitude of asking God to guide you and use you, *He will* put you in situations where He will use you. The Word of God that you have memorized and hidden in your heart will flow from your lips into someone else's heart. Once you see a transformed life, you will have just witnessed the greatest miracle that can ever take place in this lifetime. Believe me, you can never get enough of that!

My friend, Jesus wants you to become a disciple—which means a disciplined learner and follower of Him—not just a believer who sits on the sidelines. He wants you in the game all the way, and just how much you get to play is really up to you and how much you are willing to prepare. Studying God's Word, asking Him for the wisdom, knowledge, and understanding to know it, and using it for His glory are the privileges of every child of God!

17

WE NEED EACH OTHER

The New Testament has a very interesting way of describing the people who have given their lives to Jesus. We are called the body of Christ. That is right: Jesus is the Head, and we are all different members of His body.

But now God has set the members, each one of them, in the body just as He pleased. And if they were all one member, where would the body be? But now indeed there are many members, yet one body. And the eye cannot say to the hand, "I have no need of you"; nor again the head to the feet, "I have no need of you." No, much rather, those members of the body which seem to be weaker are necessary....But God composed the body... that there should be no schism in the body, but that the members should have the same **care for one another***....Now you are the body of Christ, and members individually.*
(1 Corinthians 12:18–22, 24–25, 27,
emphasis added)

Clearly, as Christians, we must understand that, in spite of our differences, we need each other to work together for Jesus. Jesus is the Head, and we are the body parts that are to move for Him on this earth. As the Head, He gives us directions, and we are to function in a way that pleases Him. This is just like a person's head telling his arms to move or his legs to walk. That's a *healthy* body, right? If we don't work together, or acknowledge one another, then the body is malfunctioning!

TRYING TO FIT

When I was a new believer, I didn't see my need for other Christians. Perhaps you don't, either. As you know, I didn't grow up in a Bible-preaching church, and I had an unusual first meeting with Jesus Christ! As a result, I didn't really understand the body of Christ—about being a part of God's people. But after we come to know Jesus, we are a part of His body, whether we realize it or not!

> It took me a few years before I understood how much I needed to become part of a local church—and how the church needed me.

It took me a few years of being alone in my faith before I began to understand how much I needed to become part of a local church. And the church needed me to be with them, because God had made me part of their family—my new family.

I must admit that, at first, just being around "these types of people"—Christians—was uncomfortable for a guy with my background, and it was very difficult for me. I may have become a Christian in my heart, but what I saw in church was all very new to me. Many of the people had been believers for years, and it seemed as if I just did not fit in very well. They were quoting Scriptures like it was so natural, and they had these "slogans" and things I had never heard. Was there a place for me?

I believe that, at the beginning, I was afraid to let them know what I had been delivered from. I didn't think they would understand. Most Christians seemed to have it all together, and I was still pretty fragile about all the changes in my life. So, I was beginning to think this whole church thing was just not for me. I couldn't get involved—it was too much. When I read all the Scriptures about being a part of the body of Christ, I wished that somehow it would work. But, for the time being, I decided to forgo church and just keep doing what I was doing and share my faith with whoever would listen.

SHARING MY STORY EVERYWHERE

Even though I was stumbling along in my opinion about the church, I was still thrilled to have been changed by Jesus Christ! I wanted to share my story with everyone I met. The amazing thing was that everywhere I went, the Holy Spirit would put people in front of me who needed Him. Excitedly, I would tell them what Jesus had done for me, and, before I knew it, I was praying for them. They would start weeping and ask Jesus into their hearts!

Over and over again, people were coming to Christ. It got to the point where I was sharing my faith with somebody almost every day, and it was awesome. This was just part of being a normal Christian, right? It never occurred to me that evangelism might be one of my spiritual gifts. I simply had no idea that each of us has been given a gift from God for the benefit of all of His people.

PUTTING BACK THE PIECES

A few years had passed since I had been discharged from the Marines. I had married Cathy, and we were raising three little boys. Because I hadn't felt comfortable at church and because of some not-so-good experiences at one of the churches we had briefly attended, I decided that I would just continue sharing Jesus wherever I went and stay away from some of these "flaky" ministers we ran into. I just didn't want to open myself or my family up to something that would lead to our getting hurt again. Obviously, this was not a good attitude, but it's honestly just where we were. And then, our lives took a dramatic turn.

You know that no matter what our cry is before God, He hears us. We needed a church body, and God led us to one. Cathy had heard about a church in a nearby community and was gently encouraging me to visit. I was skeptical when we walked in. But, as I listened carefully to the pastor, I realized that something was very different about him. He was not trying to put on a show or get cute. He was not talking about himself, and nothing seemed to be out of whack, so I just kept listening. He finished his sermon by asking for anyone who wanted prayer to step forward. Then, he requested that everyone else leave quietly and respect the people who had gone forward for prayer. Now, I could identify with that. This dedicated man told people about Jesus and then just prayed for them, focusing again on Jesus in prayer. Simple. Straightforward. Sincere.

That church became a wonderful place for us to grow in the Lord. The pastor's name is Jim Leake. (I know he wouldn't want me telling his name!) He and his wife, Becky, modeled a genuine love for God's people and showed us what it is to live a sincere, godly life. It was through their ministry that God slowly put back the pieces that the other ministers had messed up for me.

The two of them had started that church and ministered there for more than forty years before being called to a new ministry, leaving a legacy of over four decades of vibrant ministry with no scandals. In fact, the town they ministered in actually named a day after Jim; it's called "Jim Leake Day." What a godly witness to the community, and what a way to illustrate to the world the love and power of God by consistently showing concern for people and demonstrating to them that God cares for them. Pastor Jim and Becky are busier now than ever ministering in Cuba and Mexico with orphanages and marriage seminars. What a testimony for Jesus!

> Only you can bring your gift to the body of Christ to benefit others and make the body function the way it should.

DISCOVERING YOUR GIFT

As a believer in Christ, you have a gift from God that is unique for you. Only you can bring that gift to the body of Christ to benefit others and to make the body function the way that it should. If you don't attend a local church, how will your gift be used? How will you find your place in His body?

I know that most of the people who will be reading this book in the first place are going to be the type of people who are used to "going it alone." If that is your situation, I believe this is why God has you reading this chapter. God wants you to become a part of His local body of believers to help you to grow and to encourage you, as well as to give you a place to use your gifts and talents to help the local church.

A pastor is one of God's gifts to the body of Christ, and you need a pastor and the local church—we all do. Your pastor may assist you in identifying your gift for the overall growth of the local body of believers, or he may simply help you to confirm your gift. You can become a part of God's work right there in the church. Maybe you could become one of the people who encourages the pastor and comes alongside him to help him in his work. Or, if you have a gift of teaching, over time, you may teach a class of adults or children, depending on your interest. Perhaps you have a gift of encouragement to cheer others who have gone through some of the same trials you have. You may have a gift of compassion and a desire to help troubled teenagers by becoming a friend to them and just listening to them.

GET INVOLVED IN A LOCAL BODY OF BELIEVERS

Don't do what I did—don't avoid pastors and church just because some ministers are a little flaky. Cathy and I have moved to another city since those early days, but being a part of a church where we can share our gifts and our lives with other believers has remained a priority. Don't let anything stop you from getting involved with the local church and having a great relationship with the pastor. You can become a huge blessing to him and his family.

Start to develop the attitude that you want to be a giver to the local body and not just a taker. Become a sustainer and not a drainer. Be ready to serve, to give to others, and to get involved with the people because, at the end of the day, that's what Jesus came for—to bless others.

I think that one of the most universal statements Christians say in order to get out of plain, old-fashioned work or to avoid responding to a problem with common sense is "I don't feel led!" I love what my current pastor did to demonstrate this tendency. He had all the members of the congregation take little pieces of lead so they could rub their hands across them; then, nobody could say "I don't feel led" when a need was presented! We all laughed about that one.

Let me tell you about a friend in my church who responded to a need and had his life changed as a result. The church was planning a missions trip to the city of Nairobi, Kenya. This friend of mine is a contractor and a former alcoholic whom Christ has set free. He had never been on a short-term missions trip before, and he decided to go, along with a doctor, a nurse, several homemakers, and many other "ordinary" people, including myself. We were organized into three teams—a medical team, a construction team, and a ministry team.

We went on the trip and began ministering in the slums of Nairobi. You will need to go on the Internet to see pictures of how bad the living conditions are there, because words cannot properly describe the filth and devastation that millions of people have to call their homes daily. There was no running water or electricity, there were no toilets, and the people lived in ten-by-ten-foot huts with dirt floors. They had to use a plastic bag to go to the bathroom and then just throw the bag into one of the hundreds and hundreds of trash piles there. Those who are lucky live on the tops of the hills, because, when it rains, all that filth comes downhill. When you first get there, you are overwhelmed with the stench of it all. Kiberia and Mathari are the largest of the five major slums, and I was told that over a million people live in each of them. That knowledge made the mere sight of one of the slums give me a hopeless feeling.

The missionaries we worked with had to deal with this devastation every day, but I watched them behave very naturally with the people in the midst of it, as naturally as if they had been coming over to my home to help me with something or to play games with my kids. The first time I'd gone to Kenya and witnessed their ministry, it had taken me about three days to process what I was seeing. I couldn't believe it, and yet, after you see the Kenyan people trying to live a normal life as they know it, somehow, you just jump in and begin to walk alongside them, as if you have known them for many years. God's love wells up in you, and you find yourself wanting to give more and more of yourself than you ever thought possible, and you're so thankful that you have the opportunity to give to others in some small way. It changes your life forever.

On this particular trip, I was watching my friend start to build the project we were given to do. In

Nairobi, there are hundreds of children everywhere you go, and they are so happy to see you. They ran up to my friend and grabbed his arms and hands and just wanted to talk with him and have some fun. Many of these children have never seen a white person, or don't see one very often, and they were having fun feeling the hair on his arms, since people there don't have that trait, for some reason. They realized that we were not there to take something from them but to try to help them, and the kindness we received from them was enough to melt his heart.

Yes, we had a project to finish for them while we were there, but our first goal was to love them and to develop some relationships. The people want to give back to us, and the way they treat us is so humbling. Your heart is filled with such love for them that you begin to change, and I was watching my friend change before my very eyes. We were there for almost three weeks, and when you get home from a trip like that, it takes a while for you to process all that has happened. The feelings you have developed for the people make you look deep inside yourself and answer questions about yourself that you would not have considered otherwise.

On that trip, Jesus Christ showed my friend that he had gifts in his soul that God had planted there even before he was born that would minister to people who were hurting and needing someone with compassion to walk alongside them and make a difference in their lives. My friend is still a contractor, but he is also now running a ministry for people with addictions, helping hurting people to overcome their bondages.

If you have never been on a missions trip, I would encourage you to step out of your comfort zone and get involved. I can promise you, you will never be the same. You will automatically find yourself giving and cooperating with others, all for the sake of helping someone less fortunate than yourself. I know that you can go to the downtown area of any city and find people to help, and you should do that when God leads you to. But I also recommend that you take a trip with your local body of believers and become part of a team that goes somewhere totally unfamiliar to you, so that you are way outside anything you have ever done. You will find out things about yourself and others that you never would otherwise, because your surroundings are so different.

> God wants to fill you with His love and to use the gifts He planted within you before you were born.

God Will Use You in Ways You Have Never Dreamed Of

Every one of us has gifts that God Himself has put within us. God wants to use you in ways you have never dreamed of. He is just waiting to fill you with His love and to use the gifts He has planted within you before you were even born.

Will you ask Him to use you to show someone His love and to make faith come alive in someone's heart every day—yes, every day? You will be surprised to see what happens today when you give God a chance!

18

WORKPLACE AND FRIENDS

Is your workplace a challenge to your faith? Sometimes, the word *challenge* is an understatement!

I work in the business world and have to produce, just like everyone else. I have had bosses who did not care one bit about my faith, and others who went out of their way to make it very difficult for me just *because of* my faith. They would purposely "test" me to see just how serious I was about Jesus and how I would react in certain situations. They would look hard for some inconsistent area in my life and then would scornfully remark, "Yeah, he's one of those 'born-again hypocrites,' all right!"

You know, maybe they were just being convicted by the Lord in a certain area of their lives and wanted to take it out on me. Or, maybe I had sinned, and I deserved to have my Christianity rubbed in my face! Either way, whether I deserved it or not, I needed to be a man about things, live my life the best I could, and leave the results to God.

How I live my life in front of others can affect the decisions they make about God. It's an awesome gift and a great responsibility to be an ambassador for Christ. I try to imagine how the ambassador of a foreign country would prepare for a meeting with the president of the United States of America, and then I relate that to my representing God Almighty. I believe that if Christians applied this attitude to their lives, we could have much more effective testimonies before people who don't know the Lord. Hopefully, in our workplaces, we will show by our examples the difference God has made in our lives.

> In our workplaces, we need to show by our examples the difference God has made in our lives.

I believe that if my work habits are the best I can make them, if I produce more than others most of the time, if I am punctual, more prepared, and willing to work harder than most others, then I will receive respect from those around me, which is a positive reflection of my relationship with Jesus Christ. Unfortunately, many of my observations of Christians in the workplace have been discouraging. I have witnessed more laziness, unpreparedness, and excuses from Christians than I care to admit. However, when you, as a Christian, truly understand that you are to work *"as to the Lord and not to men"* (Colossians 3:23), then you will want to be the very best at your vocation, no matter what that might be.

Whatever You Do

A good friend of mine has his Ph.D. and is the president of a prestigious institution of higher learning. He related a story to me that I think you'll appreciate. He and his wife sent their children to a private school where the parents made a commitment to work a certain number of hours each month doing whatever was necessary to keep the building maintenance at a high standard. Well, the hallways needed to be scrubbed, and it happened that a hallway in the very back of the school was in the worst shape. No one else was available that day, so my friend was asked to take the bucket and mop to that back hallway and get started.

He got to the obscure hallway and had been working only a few minutes when a little voice started saying in his head, *Yeah, you have your Ph.D., and now look at you. Keep up the good work scrubbing! Hey, you missed a spot over here....* On and on it went, until he got so worked up that he was about to throw the scrub brush down the hall and walk out because he was "better than this"! To make matters worse, no one was around to see him do such a fabulous job of cleaning the back hallway!

His pride was boiling over, and he was just about to bust open. Then, he stopped and heard a different voice—a still, small voice—inside of him, saying, *"And whatever you do, do it heartily, as to the Lord and not to men"* (Colossians 3:23). He felt a surge of power come over him, and he started singing and scrubbing and polishing that floor like it was the gateway to the throne of God!

If you take this attitude to your workplace, regardless of what you do for a living, you will find that not only will you do a much better job (and perhaps get a raise or a promotion), but, more important, you will please God. And He will promote you in His time to whatever He has for you to do. Remember, the Lord promises that if you are faithful in small things, you will be given charge over much bigger things. (See Luke 16:10.)

Even If No One Is Watching!

Let me bring this concept closer to home by sharing a story that blesses me and teaches me a different lesson every time I think of it.

There was a home builder who was very successful, and his only daughter was dating a young man who worked for him. Although this young worker was a very nice guy, he had a weakness—he always wanted to take shortcuts or find the easy way out in his work. The builder saw this in him but wanted to help him overcome it. He knew that the young man's father hadn't given him a good example to follow, and, since his daughter really liked him, the builder wanted to give him an opportunity.

So, he placed the young man in charge of constructing one particular home and gave him free rein to finish it without too much involvement from him. He would make himself available if the young man had any questions, but, generally, he left him alone. The young worker, however, continued taking shortcuts in constructing the home. He simply didn't follow the best building procedures because nobody was watching over his shoulder. About six months passed, and the homes in the development went up for sale. In the meantime, the builder's daughter and the young man had become very serious in their relationship, and the father was watching this develop.

Soon after, the two became engaged and set a wedding date.

The builder was happy for the young couple, and he took them to dinner to celebrate. He also had a little lesson for his future son-in-law. "I have a gift I would like to give you," he told the young couple. He looked his employee in the eye and said, "Son, since I am sure you took extra steps in building the first home that you were in charge of, I am going to give that home to the two of you for your wedding gift!"

His daughter jumped up in excitement and threw her arms around her father's neck. Her fiancé, who had taken so many shortcuts in building the home, had to fake his excitement because he knew the shabby job he had done. Obviously, this lesson would have consequences for the young man for years to come as he tried to fix the areas of the house that he should have built correctly in the first place! Can you imagine the kind of job he would have done if he had known the house was going to be given to him and his new bride?

Remember, whatever your hands find to do, do it with all your energy as unto the Lord—that is, from your heart—and not just when someone is watching you!

SURROUND YOURSELF WITH PEOPLE WHO WILL HELP YOU GROW

It's easy to see what a person looks like on the outside. Yet, if you want to know what a person looks like on the inside, just look at his closest friends and the passion that drives his life.

Jesus was always hanging out with sinners and social outcasts, but He had a spiritual purpose for doing so. I don't think anyone can deny He was with them because He was seeking the ones who needed to be cleansed and forgiven. For most Christians, the idea of getting really close to sin before saying no is not very safe. Now that you have given your life to Christ, you need to surround yourself with people who can help you grow in your walk with God. You need to realize that we are really in a spiritual battle, and having Christian friends is one way to be victorious in that battle.

> We are in a spiritual battle, and having Christian friends is one way to be victorious in that battle.

Earlier, we talked about the need to be "good soldiers of Jesus Christ." The apostle Paul spoke often of the Christian life being a battle between good and evil forces. This is what he said in the book of Ephesians:

> *Finally, my brethren, be strong in the Lord and in the power of His might. Put on the whole armor of God, that you will be able to stand against the wiles of the devil. For we do not wrestle against flesh and blood, but against principalities, against powers, against the rulers of the darkness of this age, against spiritual hosts of wickedness in the heavenly places. Therefore take up the whole armor of God* [not just some of it, but the whole armor], *that you may be able to withstand in the evil day, and*

having done all, to stand. Stand therefore, having girded your waist with truth, having put on the breastplate of righteousness, and having shod your feet with the preparation of the gospel of peace; above all, taking the shield of faith with which you will be able to quench all the fiery darts of the wicked one. And take the helmet of salvation, and the sword of the Spirit, which is the word of God; praying always with all prayer and supplication in the Spirit, being watchful to this end with all perseverance and supplication for all the saints.

(Ephesians 6:10–18)

In other words, get ready, stay ready, and be vigilant, because your enemy the devil walks about like a roaring lion looking for someone whom he can devour. (See 1 Peter 5:8.)

Do you want that someone to be you? Of course you don't. Having Christian friends who understand the battle and have the mind-set of a soldier at war will help you to become the man or woman of God that God wants you to be. You can become an effective vessel of honor for Him to use for His glory. God longs to use all of us to build His kingdom. If you will only yield yourself to Him and prepare for that, He will use you in awesome and mighty ways.

YOUR INNER CIRCLE

We all have a part to play in this life to spread God's love to people all over the world, and preparing ourselves enables us to fulfill the roles that God has for us. Therefore, having the right circle of friends, an "inner circle," to challenge us and encourage us in God, is a key component to our spiritual success.

For example, as I am writing this chapter, I am in Las Vegas, Nevada—"Sin City," as it is promoted. But I am here as part of my career responsibilities, and with that is a spiritual purpose. I find that as I travel the world, I must put on the whole armor of God daily. Part of that armor is having two or three close friends who are sold out to God and desire to be used by Him to build His kingdom. Friends whom I am totally honest with about my walk in Christ. When I sin, when I miss the mark, I know I can share it with them, and they know they can do the same with me. We strengthen each other by our commitment to be honest with each other. We each know we are going to sin at times. It isn't that sin is an ongoing thing, but, sometimes, we just miss the mark, and we need to confess it to God and to one another in order to move on in our journeys of serving Him.

Of course, this doesn't mean that my wife and I don't share our hearts and lives together. Cathy has been the greatest friend and blessing God has given me! But men need to have other men in their lives to encourage them in God, as well, and women need to have other women in their lives to encourage them in the Lord.

I have known many great men of faith in my years as a Christian, yet I have never met a man who hasn't missed the mark in his walk with God from time to time—and it will be the same for you. But, if you are willing to be honest with one or two solid Christian friends about your spiritual life, then you will find those relationships to be a source of strength that is truly incredible.

One of my friends said to me, "Jim, when I was thinking about doing what would displease the Lord, I thought of our commitment to each other and knew I would have to be honest about it. That gave me a source of strength to say no." I know you may say, "Well, he should have known that God was watching anyway, and his commitment to God should have been enough." Maybe his commitment to God *should* have been enough, but we are mere men who are made from the dust of the earth. (See Psalm 103:13–14.) The fact is that we just need to strengthen and encourage one another. The Bible reminds us, *"Exhort ["encourage" NIV] one another daily, while it is called 'Today,' lest any of you be hardened through the deceitfulness of sin"* (Hebrews 3:13).

> We are made from the dust of the earth, and we need to strengthen and encourage one another.

I remember there was a well-known preacher who fell into sin. When he was asked how and why it could happen to him, he answered, "Who was I supposed to go to?" In other words, he had come to a place in his walk where he believed that somehow he was above being accountable to other men because he was sharing the gospel with millions.

Remember the saying, "You are who you are when you do what you do when no one you know is looking at you!" Trust me, having some friends in your inner circle whom you can be totally honest with will help you to progress a great deal in your faith journey.

19

THE JOURNEY

I started this faith journey on December 27, 1971, and I never could have imagined how God had it all planned out for me. My three best friends, God the Father, Jesus Christ, and the Holy Spirit, have proven to be more exciting to follow than anything this world could possibly have to offer.

The entire purpose for my writing this book is to share with you how this awesome God has picked me up, washed me in the blood of Christ, forgiven me of all my sins, and let me know how much He loves to fellowship with me. I know better than anyone else my shortcomings, and yet the faithfulness of God has been the one constant thing in my life. Even when I have turned my back on God, He has stood by me and gently prodded me back to Himself. Then, once again, I am overwhelmed by His forgiveness and surrounded by His love, which puts me back on track.

Even though you have now read through many of the things I wanted to share, I still don't know where you are today with your understanding of God and

His love for you. But I do know how God feels about *you*, because He never changes; *"Jesus Christ is the same yesterday, today, and forever"* (Hebrews 13:8).

People often quote John 3:16; you even see people holding up signs with this Bible reference at sporting events. But the reality is that it remains true for all of us: God loved the world (including you) so much that He sent His only Son, Jesus Christ, to die for you. If you were the only person in the entire world, Jesus would have died just for you. You are never beyond the reach of God and His love for you, no matter what you've done. It doesn't matter if you've tried God a hundred times and kept failing and failing.

> You are never beyond the reach of God and His love for you, no matter what you've done.

I can't emphasize enough that His love for us is not dependent on what we do but on what Jesus did on the cross for us. If you still haven't asked Jesus to come into your life, you can pray this prayer with me right now:

> Lord Jesus, please forgive me and cleanse me of all my sin. Please come into my heart right now, forgive me, and help me to live for You, because I cannot do it without You. Please, God, place Your Holy Spirit within me and make me Your own.

My heartfelt prayer for you is that you would sense the very presence of God right now, and that you would start every day on your knees before Him. He will take you on an incredible journey, because that's His promise to all of us.

FINALLY...STAND!

Remember how we talked about the armor of God in the last chapter? In Ephesians 6, Paul gave us a powerful description of the armor we need in order to fight the attacks of our enemy—the devil—on this earth.

First, Paul encouraged us to *"be strong in the Lord and in the power of His might"* (verse 10). He reminds us of the importance to *"put on the whole armor of God, that you may be able to stand against the wiles of the devil"* (verse 11). This was also a caution that it is not *people* we should be fighting in this world, but Satan and his tricks: *"For we do not wrestle against flesh and blood* [that is, not against human beings], *but against principalities, against powers, against the rulers of the darkness of this age, against spiritual hosts of wickedness in the heavenly places"* (verse 12). We may not understand all there is to know about the devil, but we know that he is the author of all the wickedness on this earth! *"Therefore take up the whole armor of God, that you may be able to withstand in the evil day, and having done all, to stand"* (verse 13).

What do we do after we have put on the whole armor and prayed to God for His help? We believe His Word, and we *stand* in our faith!

There will be a day when you will have to just stand there after putting on your armor, and you will need to "fight the good fight of faith" without another person's help, placing all your trust and confidence in almighty God to come to your rescue. All hell with its fury will seem to be raging at you, in your mind, in your body, in every aspect of your life. Even your loved ones, your closest friends, everything, may come knocking on your door to claim your faith in God. What is your job on that day? To *stand* in faith and trust God to get you through this time of testing.

> Remember that it's never your strength on which you are standing, but always on God's strength and your faith in Him.

Remember that it's never your strength on which you are standing, but always on God's strength and your faith in Him. Also, remember that it's the faith God gave to you, not something you work up. It's faith in God that He will *never* let you down. As you are challenged in some aspect of your life, He will prove to you once again that only He is almighty God, and He will fight your battles for you. He will take you to the front lines of battle and show you His power, if you will let Him work in your life.

STANDING UP TO THE BULLY

When my sons were young, they had a chance to stand up to a neighborhood bully. My oldest son, who was about ten years old at the time, walked slowly into the house one day, and I knew something was wrong. After some persuading from me, he finally spoke up.

"Dad, Bill is outside. He wants to fight me, and I'm afraid."

Now, I was a young dad at the time, and I may not recommend this course of action for you and your children, but it was a good lesson for all of us that day. Bill, the neighborhood bully, had been pushing the neighborhood kids around for a long time, and I knew my son had to get over this fear. Instinctively, I knew that Bill was not as tough as he was acting; it's just that no one was standing up to him.

I got on my knees, looked my son in the eyes, and asked him, "Do you trust me?" Wide-eyed, he answered, "Yes, Dad, of course I do." "Do you think I would lie to you?" I asked next. "No, Dad," he said, shaking his head solemnly, "you wouldn't." So I told him that I believed Bill was just a big mouth, and that if he stood up to him, he would just crumble and leave him alone. Bill was just going to keep pushing him around until he stood up to him.

"I want you to go outside, and if Bill starts this stuff again, I want you to just push him in the chest. Tell him you have had enough and that if he doesn't stop it, you will finish it!"

Well, I saw three things happening with my son. One, fear was trying to jump all over him. Two, there was a little excitement way back in his eyes (emphasis on "way back"). Three, he was looking at me like I was crazy! I assured him that I would be watching out the window and would be there to help him if he needed it. He paced back and forth for a while, and then he got a determined look on his face, and he said, "Okay, Dad, I'm on my way!"

Well, now, I really felt like a jerk! Boy, was I glad that my wife wasn't home! She never would have gone for this. (Cathy and I still talk and laugh about it to this day.) But I also felt just a little bit excited. Every guy knows what it's like to be so scared of someone that you become almost crippled with fear. As his father, I knew this was a point in my son's life when he needed to stand and not take it anymore. I had always taught my kids that fights were foolish and didn't prove anything, so they should never start one. But I also knew that standing up for yourself is something entirely different and that this could be a defining moment for him, at ten years of age.

As I watched carefully out the window, my son walked into the backyard with his little brother, and, sure enough, Bill came over, acting tough. He started to bully them, making threats like he always did. This time, however, my oldest son stood in front of Bill, pushed him in the chest, and yelled something in his face like, "I've had enough of you! I'm sick of you trying to push me around for no reason. If you want to fight, come on, let's go; I'll punch you right in your mouth!" Bill just stood there and turned as white as a ghost! (Boy, was I relieved!) Then, something happened I'd never thought about. My younger son grabbed a little plastic bat, smacked Bill in the legs, and said, "Yeah, leave us alone; we're not doing anything to you!"

Bill just put his head down and apologized for acting like that. Sure enough, the boys shook hands and just started playing like kids do. I was so relieved and glad that it had ended that way, but I knew that this was a day my sons would never forget. A day they just had to stand and believe what their father was telling them to do.

TOUGH TIMES COME

There are tough moments we all have to deal with. Tough times come. Now, I don't want to compare the trials we go through as adults to what my boys faced more than twenty years ago with a neighborhood bully. But I believe that, with even more love than I had looking out the window at my sons, our heavenly Father is looking out the window of heaven at us all the time. There is never a moment when He is not taking care of us and watching over us. Life's difficulties happen to us all, and it's in those times when we really learn of our heavenly Father's love.

> Life's difficulties happen to us all, and it's in those times when we really learn of our heavenly Father's love.

God is more concerned about our character than our comfort. The Bible tells us that Jesus Himself *"learned obedience by the things which He suffered"* (Hebrews 5:8). Why do we think we are excluded from that? God will never leave us or forsake us (see, for example, Deuteronomy 31:6, 8), and we can draw our strength from that truth. His promise is this: *"As your days, so shall your strength be"* (Deuteronomy 33:25). In plain words, if God has given us another day, then He has promised to see us through it—not necessarily to stop the immediate pain, but to see us through it.

I have often heard people express this thought: "Sometimes God calms the storm, and sometimes He lets it rage and calms His child." Either way, God has promised that He will be with us every step of the way.

This is not the time to crumble under the weight of the difficulties warring against you. This is the time for you to truly stand and watch your heavenly Father fight your battles for you. The Bible says that if we faint in the day of adversity, our strength is small. (See Proverbs 24:10.) Don't let that be said of you. Our faith is the substance, or proof, of the things we cannot see. (See Hebrews 11:1.) Even if you can't see the answer yet, *stand in Him*!

THE LORD OUR SHEPHERD

As I said, my desire to write this book was to personally give you the account of how almighty God came to my rescue. I wanted you to know that the very heartbeat of God is to have a close personal relationship with you. It's His desire for you to know just how much He loves you, regardless of what you've done or who you've become.

God created you in His image, and He is drawing you to Himself. Psalm 23 reads like this:

The LORD is my shepherd;
I shall not want.
He makes me to lie down in green pastures;
He leads me beside the still waters.
He restores my soul;
He leads me in the paths of righteousness
For His name's sake.
Yea, though I walk through the valley of
   the shadow of death,
I will fear no evil;
For you are with me;

Your rod and Your staff, they comfort me.
You prepare a table before me in the
*   presence of my enemies;*
You anoint my head with oil;
My cup runs over.
Surely goodness and mercy shall follow me
All the days of my life;
And I will dwell in the house of the LORD
Forever.

If you look closely at all these verses, the One doing all the work is God. He is the One who makes you to lie down. He is the One who places you next to the still waters. He is the One who restores your soul. He is the One who leads you, comforts you, and defends you. He is the One initiating everything, so don't try to wait until you get things cleaned up! He is the One who wants to love you and protect you. All He requires is that you yield to Him and ask Him to forgive you. Can you humble yourself before the almighty Creator?

"SPARKING GEMS"

While my mom was alive, she asked me what she could do for me. She just wanted to be a blessing to me in some small way, and I kept telling her, "Mom, you don't have to do anything for me," but she kept insisting, so I asked her to do this: "Mom, when you get a few moments, please sit down in front of a cassette recorder and just speak into the recorder the particular moments in your life when God did something very special for you. Please, speak into the recorder the things that have meant the most to you in all of your life. The things that you would want everyone who ever knew you to hear from you when you were long gone. Those 'sparkling gems' you would like to leave behind for all of your family to have forever to listen to."

The reason I asked her to do this was that, over many, many years, my mom had developed a prayer life in which she would spend hours every day interceding for the cares and concerns of others—not just her family members, but also hundreds and hundreds of people. She would have lists and lists of people, many whom she would never meet personally, and she considered it a privilege to come before God and pray for their needs.

The other thing she would do during these times was simply worship God. It was a very common thing to walk into her home and find her either on her knees or at her small dining room table, singing and praising almighty God. She just loved to worship God. She truly was a selfless person; she gave and gave and gave of herself for the needs of others. You would never hear a bad word about anyone come out of her mouth. Whenever I would comment negatively about someone, her automatic response would be something like, "Oh, Jimmy, you just don't know what that person may be going through," or "Jim, let's just spend a few minutes right now and pray and ask God to touch that person and help him through this situation."

Sometimes, I would get frustrated with her and think she just didn't get it. *This guy was being a jerk, and he needed to wise up,* I would think to myself, or I would just say some other unkind thing about someone. (I am sure you've never said anything unkind, right?)

Then, after my mom died, I received a voicemail message from my sister Lynn that said she had something very important to tell me. Well, I had forgotten all about asking my mom to record herself speaking onto a cassette and tell me about the "sparkling gems" in her life. So, I called Lynn, wondering what she wanted to talk about.

She told me that she'd been going through Mom's things when she'd seen a cassette player on Mom's desk, which she had used to listen to worship music. Then, next to the cassette player, Lynn saw a tape with my name on it. She put it in the player, and when she pressed play, she was completely overcome with emotion because it was my mom's voice talking to me about all the precious moments in her life. She was recounting the happy times, some sad times, and some special family moments that would just make you cry to listen to her describe them. But the best stories were about the things that God had done for her. The times when He'd made her to lie down beside quiet waters. The times when He'd comforted her. The picture was unfolding of how He was her Good Shepherd.

Mom spoke these things in her quiet, soft voice, and then she told me about the moments when God had done something miraculous for my brother Jack or Bill or Mark or Joe, my sister Jane or Isobel or Lynn. Then, she told me some promise God gave us in His Word and how she would hang on to that promise, and how, when she was in the depths of despair, that promise would minister to her and lift her from the despair. She recounted some times that were very moving and miraculous for our family.

Can you imagine discovering a recording from your mom, after she had recently passed away, in which she was even now speaking directly to you? Can you imagine your mom sitting quietly in her bedroom, with no one else around, telling you about some of the most special moments in her life as a mother who'd had eight children? Can you picture your mom letting you see into her relationship with God when He was speaking with her, and the holiness of those moments? I wept like a baby and laughed and shook my head and pondered all these things, and I have listened to that tape many, many times.

> God has a word for every situation, and if you will seek Him, He will reveal Himself to you, because that is His promise.

I just finished listening to this tape again, and the overriding theme of all that my mom had to say to me was this: The Lord truly is our Shepherd and will do all those things for us that are listed in Psalm 23. Our God is not just a mighty God, but He is *the almighty God*, and He personally wants to bless you and bring you into His presence. He will never allow anything in your life that He will not give you the strength to go through. His Word is the most important thing in this world, and you need to fall in love with it and make it personal to you. God has a word for every situation, and if you will seek Him, He will reveal Himself to you, because that is His promise.

My mom told me that she remembered the times when she would come to our home and hear me praying in the early morning hours, and that the most important thing I could ever do in this life was to be before God, worshipping Him and interceding for the needs of others. *She told me never to stop praying like that because it is the secret to living a victorious life for Christ.*

She told me many more personal things on that tape, and maybe someday I'll have the privilege of writing a book about leaving a legacy like that, or maybe I'll run into you somewhere and we can sit down and talk about it. But, for now, please read the last chapter of this book, because it really is the most important decision ever made for you.

20

THE GREAT DECISION

One of the greatest decisions ever made was one that was made for you and for me.

The Bible tells us of the night Jesus cried out to His Father in the garden of Gethsemane: *"And being in agony, He prayed more earnestly. Then His sweat became like great drops of blood falling down to the ground"* (Luke 22:44). This scene in the garden took place just before Jesus surrendered to the Roman guards. I say "surrendered" rather than "was captured," because He willingly allowed them to come and take Him into captivity.

That night, Jesus led Peter, James, and John to a special grove in the garden and asked them to pray with Him. They were to remain there while He went away *"about a stone's throw"* (verse 41) so He could be alone with His Father. It was an intense time of prayer right before His crucifixion. In His prayers, Jesus cried out to His Father, *"Father, if it is Your will, take this cup away from Me; nevertheless not My will, but Yours, be done"* (verse 42).

> If only we could truly understand how much God wants to have fellowship with us, what a difference it would make in our lives!

One thing we can see from Jesus' agony in the garden is that He really needed to be alone with His Father. He knew that there was no other place to find true peace and comfort. Jesus had an intimate relationship with His Father, and He knew that His Father always listened to Him and wanted to have fellowship with Him. (If only we could truly understand how much God wants to have fellowship with us, what a difference it would make in our lives!)

But as Jesus cried out to His Father, He asked three times if the cup of His suffering could pass from Him. (See Matthew 26:36–44.) We are not told exactly what God said back to Him, but we know that Jesus always submitted to His Father's will. Therefore, whatever God said to Him, Jesus willingly accepted. He said, *"Nevertheless not My will, but Yours, be done,"* and then He willingly surrendered to the Roman guards. We can assume that the Father reminded Jesus that the plan was the cross—for our redemption. After all, that is the entire reason Jesus came to the earth in the first place.

THE CONVERSATION

I am always overwhelmed when I think of the conversation that Jesus had with His Father. There He was in the garden, late at night, on His knees, alone, praying under the great stress of the moment.

Obviously, He knew that He was about to face one of the most painful forms of punishment that the society of the time had to offer. He had a human body, so He knew the excruciating pain He was about to endure. He also knew that if He wanted to, He could ask His Father to send more than twelve legions of angels to rescue Him from His captors (see Matthew 26:53), but He also knew the plan.

Jesus experienced more pressure than any person could bear, and the agonizing stress caused great drops of blood to pour from His sweat glands. Yet, instead of allowing that agony to cause Him to say, "No, I am not going through with this," He willingly surrendered to the Father and silently allowed the guards to take Him away.

The book of Isaiah states,

He was oppressed and He was afflicted, yet He opened not His mouth; He was as a lamb to the slaughter, and as a sheep before its shearers is silent, so He opened not His mouth. (Isaiah 53:7)

The conversation between the Father and the Son that night was the most important conversation that has ever taken place in the history of the world. During this conversation, Jesus voluntarily made the final decision to surrender to the Father's plan to die for the sins of us all. This particular night, with all the pressure of hell coming against Him, Jesus made the decision to suffer once and for all for you and for me and for all of humanity. It was this decision, this night, that would change eternity, and it all came from the conversation Jesus had with His Dad, His heavenly Father.

Again, I wonder what it was that His Dad said to Him. How was it delivered to Him? What type of voice did God the Father use to speak to His Son? How did Jesus feel as He looked squarely at this truth and surrendered to it? *"For God so loved the world that He gave His only begotten Son, that whoever believes in Him should not perish but have everlasting life"* (John 3:16).

Obviously, before Jesus ever came down to earth, He and His Father had talked about His coming into the world and dying for the sins of humanity. Together, They knew what the overall plan was in order for human beings to be saved and have the right to enter heaven. They knew every step that would be taken by Jesus and everyone else in history because They are divine, They are supreme, They are sovereign, They are all-powerful, and They are omnipotent.

A MOST AMAZING NIGHT

But Jesus had to be fully human, too, in order to suffer on the cross for you and for me. And that is why we are taking a close look at that most amazing night.

> What greater demonstration of love could Father and Son make that night than for Jesus to freely lay down His life for you and for me?

God the Father and Jesus the Son had a conversation about you and me and the sacrifice that had to be made in order for us to be forgiven, so that we could spend eternity in heaven. And in spite of what They knew it would cost Them, They willingly made the decision. They wanted to rescue us from the power of Satan and all the powers of darkness and to be able to write our names in the Lamb's Book of Life. (See Revelation 21:27.) What greater demonstration of love could Father and Son make that night than for Jesus to freely lay down His life for you and for me?

Jesus knew no sin, but He became sin for us. *"For He* [God] *made Him* [Jesus] *who knew no sin to be sin for us, that we might become the righteousness of God in Him"* (2 Corinthians 5:21). Jesus never sinned; He had never been separated from His Father because of sin. But now, He would be hung on a cross, be separated from His Father as He took on our sins, shed His blood, and give His life because of the decision that was made that night.

That final decision—that conversation—was the turning point for all of history! It was during that night of such agony that He suffered until He sweat blood. The medical community calls this condition of sweating blood *hematohidrosis*. On rare occasions, when someone comes under tremendous stress, the blood vessels constrict, and then, as the anxiety passes, the blood vessels dilate to the point of rupture and the blood leaks into the sweat glands. Since the sweat glands are producing a lot of sweat, the blood is pushed to the surface, coming out as droplets of blood mixed with water and sweat.

The real stress of the moment for Jesus was not all the pain He was about to go through but the trauma of taking the guilt of all of humanity's sins upon Himself. Yes, your sins and mine are what He died for. Your sins and mine are what He sweat great drops of blood for. Your sins and mine are what the conversation between the Son and the Father was all about that night in the garden of Gethsemane. Yes, you and I are the reason Jesus willingly laid down His life and suffered the death of the cross.

When it's put in this light, we can see clearly just how wide and how deep and how long God's love for humanity is (see Ephesians 3:17–19), that He desires that no one would perish, no, not one! (See 2 Peter 3:9.) I'm going to repeat John 3:16 because it is the truth: *"God so loved the world that He gave His only begotten Son, that whoever believes in Him should not perish but have everlasting life."*

GOD WAS JUSTIFIED

What I am about to share with you now wasn't possible for me to talk about until I'd first shared about Jesus' loving decision in the garden of Gethsemane. I also cannot share it without tears in my eyes. Do you realize that because of my sin, God would have been justified to send me to hell for all eternity—and that the same is true for you?

When I share my faith with people, many times, they will say to me, "Jim, if your God is so loving and kind, how can He condemn a soul to hell and justify Himself in doing so?" Or, they might respond, "Jim, you can't be serious. You can't really think that God is going to send someone to hell for eternity just because he doesn't believe the way you do." Or, "Jim, you can't be that naïve and narrow-minded to actually say and believe that Jesus Christ is the only way of salvation and the only way to God!"

Yes, I can say that and believe it. But it doesn't mean that God wants to send anyone to hell; it doesn't mean that He won't reach out to us in love, just as He did to me so many years ago. God gives us so many opportunities to hear His plan of salvation and receive it into our hearts. He doesn't choose for a man or woman to spend eternity without Him. People choose it when they reject God's plan for their redemption.

I say this to you with a very humble heart, but I believe the reason you are reading this book is because of the conversation Jesus had with His Father that night in the garden. He is providing you with another chance to accept His salvation. God loves you so much. He never intended for you to be separated from Him. He is reaching out to you again right now. He is knocking on the door of your heart. It's no coincidence that everywhere you go, you feel this tugging in your heart for something more in life.

> God loves you so much. He never intended for you to be separated from Him, and He is providing you with another chance to accept His salvation.

What you are truly longing for is a relationship with your heavenly Father, and He is longing to have the same with you. He is the initiator of this relationship, and it can happen because of the decision Jesus made in the garden that night long ago. God doesn't want *anyone* to perish. God made you, and He loves you. He loves you so much that He is trying once again to communicate this to you right now. What is stopping you from receiving His gift of eternal life? Could it be that you want things on your own terms? Could it be that since you are successful and educated, you think you are above it all?

Can the clay say to the potter, "No, I want it done my way"? (See Isaiah 29:16; 45:9.) What is man that God is even mindful of him? (See Psalm 8:4.) Don't you realize that God made us from the dust of the earth and that, one day, we will return to it? Again, I would respectfully say to you that God doesn't send anyone to hell; people choose that themselves. God cannot be anything but perfectly right in all things. He is supremely divine. No, God never intends for any man or woman to go to hell; He just knows it will happen because some people insist on doing things their own ways.

I know that, in holding this view, I am in the minority, especially among people of means. I know that some people with money forget about the end of their lives because they are flying high right now and enjoying the finest things this life has to offer. But, my friend, I am begging you not to laugh this off. A day will arrive when you will come up empty. A day will arrive when you will encounter Jesus Christ face-to-face. A day will arrive when God will ask you only one question: "What have you done with the sacrifice that My Son made for you after the decision He made that night in the garden?" What will your answer be?

The Bible clearly states that *"at the name of Jesus every knee* [will] *bow, of those in heaven, and of those on earth, and of those under the earth, and... every tongue* [will] *confess that Jesus Christ is Lord, to the glory of God the Father"* (Philippians 2:10–11). The only question is, will you bow your knee on this side of the grave, or when it will be too late?

Do you understand now why Jesus' decision in the garden of Gethsemane was one of the most important decisions ever made? Will you make your decision today to surrender to Christ, just the way He surrendered to His captors to die for you and for me?

My heart's cry for you and for all your loved ones is that you will understand just how much God loves you and wants to have fellowship with you. He longs to walk with you and for you to walk with Him. Today can be your day of decision.

With a sincere heart before God, pray this simple prayer:

> Father God, thank You for the decision that Jesus made for me that night. I know I am a sinner, and I ask that You would forgive me and cleanse me of all of my sins. Jesus, please come into my heart and be my Lord and my Savior forever. Amen.

A FINAL WORD

I hope this book has been a blessing to you. My desire is that God would use it to encourage you and draw you closer to Him. As I said earlier, I have walked with Him for forty years at this point in my life, and His love and kindness to me are new every morning. *"Because of the Lord's great love we are not consumed, for his compassions never fail. They are new every morning; great is your faithfulness"* (Lamentations 3:22–23 NIV).

I have shared my heart with you in these pages. I pray that you will stay surrendered to the Lord all the days of your life. Never forget these powerful words; keep them close to your own heart, and share them with those around you:

> *If you confess with your mouth the Lord Jesus and believe in your heart that God has raised Him from the dead, you will be saved. For with the heart one believes unto righteousness, and with the mouth confession is made unto salvation. For the Scripture says, "Whoever believes on Him will not be put to shame." For there is no distinction between Jew and Greek, for the same Lord over all is rich to all who call upon Him. For* **"whoever calls on the name of the Lord shall be saved."**
>
> (Romans 10:9–13, emphasis added)

Please call on Him today, right now. Jesus loves you, and so do I.

Thanks, and God bless you,

Jim Maxim

About the Author

Jim Maxim and his wife, Cathy, have been involved in inner-city ministry for over twenty-five years. They have also recently formed Acts413, a ministry to pastors and Christian leaders in all walks of life, encouraging them to renew the vital "secret place" of prayer in their lives. Jim serves on the boards of People for People and World Impact, and he is the chair of The Hope Center, an inner-city crisis pregnancy center. He has been involved with teaching pastors and ministering to children in the slums of Kenya while working with various missions organizations in Africa.

Jim is founder and president of Maxim Automotive and MaximTrak Technologies. MaximTrak designs, develops, and deploys state-of-the-art technologies to help automotive retailers and OEMs manage and improve profitability and compliance within their sales and finance departments.

Jim and Cathy live in the suburbs of Philadelphia and have three sons, three daughters-in-law, and three grandchildren.

Acts413
P.O. Box 628
Southeastern, PA 19399
www.acts413.net • 610-721-1010